The Adventurous Life of Winston Churchill

THE
ADVENTUROUS LIFE OF
WINSTON CHURCHILL

By

GEOFFREY BOCCA

JULIAN MESSNER, INC.

New York

Cartoons on pages 65, 94, 138, 158 reproduced with special permission from *Punch*. Endpaper, reproduced with special permission from Odhams Press Limited, was specially drawn by David Low for *Illustrated's Churchill Supplement,* November 20, 1954.

Published by Julian Messner, Inc.
8 West 40 Street, New York 18

Published simultaneously in Canada
by The Copp Clark Publishing Co. Limited

Printed in the United States of America

Library of Congress Catalog Card No. 58-11843

Contents

Illustrations

Part I

The Young Rebel

John Churchill, first Duke of Marlborough. Winston Churchill's father was the third son of the seventh Duke. Had the ninth Duke died childless Winston would have inherited the title. The present Duke is the tenth, born in 1897.

1

The Young Rebel

WINSTON LEONARD SPENCER CHURCHILL ARRIVED IN 1874 JUST, IT seemed, to crown his father's year of achievement. Lord Randolph Churchill, at the age of twenty-five, had entered Parliament in February of that year after a riotous election. In April he had married a formidably beautiful American girl of twenty, Jeanette Jerome. In the summer he rose before the House and made a maiden speech on which Disraeli commented approvingly in a note to the Queen. And on November 30th Winston was born, a gloomy red-headed child whom the family had not expected until some time in January of the following year.

"Born prematurely," it said in the *Times,* a fact so appropriate to all the events which were to accumulate in the child's life that it has occasioned hilarity even in the most august of his biographers. This descendant of the Dukes of Marlborough was born at Blenheim Palace, the ancestral home, shrine to the glory of British arms and the splendor of her greatest soldier, John Churchill, the first Duke—320 rooms of treasures and trophies, of portraits of Marlboroughs illustrious and indifferent. Outside there were 2,700 acres of park land and woodland and arches of triumph, a large expanse of playground for a child, especially a child with no one to play with. For Winston's parents were more than a little preoccupied with the society around them. "We seemed to live in a whirl of gaieties and excitement," Jennie wrote in her memoirs. "Many were the delightful balls I went to . . . lasting to five in the morning. Masked balls were much the vogue . . ."

Aerofilms Ltd. from Pi:

Blenheim Palace.

When one goes to bed at dawn one's waking hours seldom cross those of an infant's, but this was the nineteenth century—England's century—and Englishmen found themselves compelled by an irresistible momentum to make the most of it before the twentieth century opened its door. There was peace in the world, and Englishmen kept it—English soldiery in red jackets, English justice in full-bottomed wigs, English bluejackets on the high seas and the Union Jack waving in the Himalayas and in darkest Africa, across all five' continents, over black, brown, yellow and white. Such an Empire the world had never seen, this Empire into which Winston was born; and from its outposts into London and Liverpool docks came the spices and riches of the world, a dazzling torrent of gold for the financing of great projects, for the building of town and country mansions, the pleasures of the ballroom, the card table, the turf and the water, to buy immortality or go to the devil.

14

The Young Rebel

There was another side to the coin. Seventy miles away from the nursery bedroom of Blenheim Palace in which a red-topped infant slept was London, where other children with faces as wizened as monkeys waited in the gaslit streets until midnight, for their mothers and fathers to fall out of the public houses. London was rollicking, it was rich and it was rough, redolent of gin and jellied eels, champagne and port, and bursting with confidence, with mashers in the music halls and Cockneys on the Heath, singing:

"How do you like London? How do you like town?
  How do you like the Strand, dear, now Temple Bar's pulled down?
  How do you like the lah-di-dah, the toothpick and the crutch?
  How did you get these trousers on, and do they hurt you much?"

Benjamin Disraeli had replaced William Gladstone as Prime Minister. Queen Victoria was slowly recovering from her grief at Prince Albert's death thirteen years earlier. It is all so long ago, longer than even the oldest can truly remember. In the same *London Times* that announced Winston's birth was announced the death of gentlemen born before the French Revolution. Some old Oxfordshire gaffers who looked on Winston in his carriage had fought as youths against Napoleon.

Across the Channel Paris was still pulling itself together from the Prussian siege which had reduced the citizens to a diet of rats. The Tuileries, the Hotel de Ville and the Palais de Justice were shells from the fires of the 1871 Commune and its aftermath. Across the Atlantic the United States still mourned a million dead Americans from the war that had ended a decade before, and the South was a desert of bitterness and nostalgia.

England swept on in a sea of gold and complacency, and none strained for the future more eagerly than Winston's father. True, Lord Randolph's allowance from his father was a modest one and he welcomed the income of £6,000 a year which his wife brought

Lord and Lady Randolph Churchill.

with her, for the life of a gentleman was an expensive one, and to compromise with one's tastes and social obligations was unthinkable. In spite of some financial difficulties, however, Randolph with his American bride and unexpected scion was, above all others, the nation's coming man.

To look at him was startling—small with protruding brandy-ball eyes, large ears and enormous walrus moustaches, all sticking out of a small head and making him look somewhat Martian, but withal a dandy, engaging, attractive to women. The nineteenth century had produced some undistinguished Churchills, but the impulsive Randolph created a feeling, thrilling to Englishmen with their dynastic sense, that here was a true descendant of England's greatest soldier. Jennie was a perfect match. She was one of the daughters of Leonard Jerome of New York, a flamboyant newspaper proprietor, gambler and sportsman who chased money and women and accepted their capture or escape with equal aplomb. Jennie had in her a touch of Iroquois Indian blood. She was flashingly beautiful, dark,

16

Leonard W. Jerome.

The Prince of Wales (later Edward VII).

Creole-looking, and she was in the habit of wearing a tortoise-shell comb at the back of her chignon. There was, according to an admirer, "more of the panther than the woman in her look," and she was the perfect politician's wife: intelligent, amusing, with a flair for telling somewhat risqué stories, and she played the piano charmingly.

They were, indeed, an exciting couple and English political observers, always conscious of natural genius, forecast that Lord Randolph could end his career nowhere but at No. 10 Downing Street.

Then when little Winston was scarcely twelve months old everything changed. The Prince of Wales engaged in a private argument with Lord Randolph's brother, Lord Blandford, over a lady, and was furious when Randolph rashly but honorably intervened for his brother. The Prince declared angrily he would never again cross the threshold of anyone who entertained the Churchills. Thus with a sentence, the shutters of society closed on the young couple. For Randolph the blow was shattering. Society flowed as the blood in his own veins and he now found himself ostracized by everyone to whom he would normally turn for association and companionship. Jennie expressed their distress gently in her memoirs. "Most people in the course of a lifetime," she wrote, "get to know the real value of the Mammon of Unrighteousness, but few learn the lesson so early."

The vendetta dragged on for eight years and then died. English society was exasperated at having to walk a tightrope between the Prince and one of its most fascinating members, and the Prince, for his part, became bored with the quarrel. He was not a vindictive man. Basically he liked Randolph and missed his exuberance. He made the first gesture of friendship, which Randolph accepted thankfully and the breach was healed.

All the time Winston was growing up, a solemn, unhappy-looking little boy whose pictures rarely show a smile. When he was six he acquired a baby brother, John, but the difference in ages was too

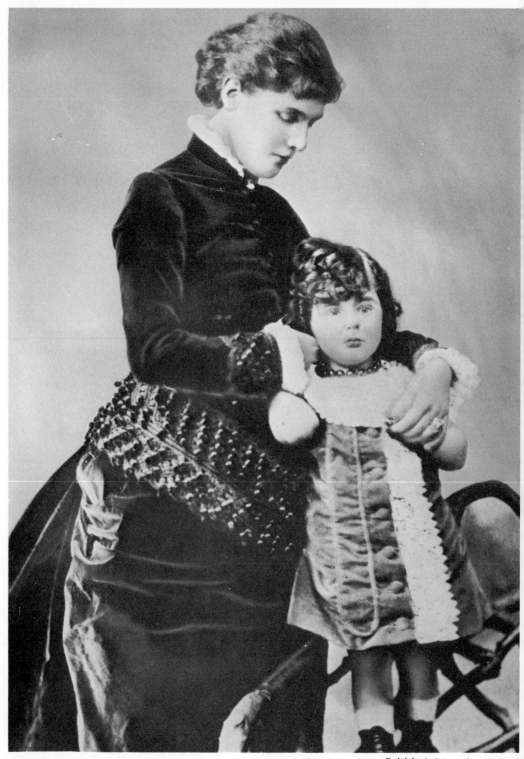

One of the earliest pictures of Winston Churchill, with his mother.

much for companionship. He was aware of his father's gloom and his mother's disappointment over an existence that had turned so abruptly from fairy gold to dead leaves. He adored his father and was dazzled by his mother who "shone for me like the evening star. I love her dearly but at a distance. She always seemed to me a fairy princess." When the bar on the Churchills was lifted the family atmosphere brightened, but the big difference it made to little Winston was that he saw even less of his parents than before, and fell back for affection on his nurse, Mrs. Everest, whom he was to regard with devotion for the rest of her life.

Lord Randolph had taken a house in Connaught Place and had it installed with electric light, the first private home in London to acquire such an innovation. He then selected a boarding school at Ascot for Winston. There the boy was beaten so severely that not even the passage of the years enabled him to recall it with anything but the thinnest humor, and friends in later years were sometimes taken aback by the most uncharacteristic venom with which Winston spoke of education and schooling. He found what appeared to be his natural level at the bottom of the class. Fortunately Lady Randolph sensed her son's unhappiness, and she took him away to a kinder school in Brighton, where he was better treated but otherwise showed little improvement. It must have seemed to him that those who loved him saw him so little, while those around him were endlessly hostile. Miss Eva Moore, the distinguished actress, teaching him to dance found him "a small red-headed pupil, the naughtiest boy in his class. I used to think he was the naughtiest boy in the world." Actually he was just a small boy in revolt against authority, that most hopeless of all causes.

There were happier moments. Queen Marie of Rumania in her memoirs recalls childhood meetings with Winston. Marie was the daughter of the Duke of Edinburgh and the Grand Duchess Marie Alexandrovna of Russia. Winston, a few months older than she, was a frequent visitor at the Duke's home, Osborne Cottage on the estate

The young rebel.

of Queen Victoria. Marie remembered him as snub-nosed, freckled and impudent, and they fell in love, Winston declaring before witnesses that he would marry her when he grew up. They were ten years old. "I don't think Mamma considered that he improved our manners," Queen Marie added reflectively. It was her first adventure in love and, presumably, Winston's.

But there was always the misery of a school which dispirited and debilitated him. The doctor said the boy was delicate. When the time came to make the transition from prep school to public school Lord Randolph decided, in some disappointment, that his son should go, not to Eton, the family school, which is on a river, but to Harrow, which is built on a hill.

Even that was not so easy for this strange problem child. The Harrow entrance examinations were not very difficult, because what Harrow wants from a boy is rarely academic distinction, but Winston could not even pass tests which were little more than formalities. Dr. Welldon, the headmaster, was not content. He could not believe that a man of Lord Randolph's stature could possess such an utterly witless son. The boy *had* to have something. He examined Winston's papers himself and became increasingly gloomy in the process but accepted Winston anyway, an intuitive decision which he probably would have been unable to explain even to himself, and Winston was admitted as the lowest boy in the last class. There he comfortably stayed.

He was as rebellious as ever but too young to understand what against, except that the whole world appeared to conspire to keep him from his father and mother and piled on him tasks which he saw no reason or satisfaction in performing. He hated Latin and Greek, hated team games like football and cricket, but he swam strongly and rode well, having ridden horses since childhood. Had he been a more sensitive child he would have been broken by the system, which does not tolerate rebels gladly. As it was he simply became a more accomplished rebel. In the school magazine he wrote some items criticizing certain aspects of the system and the masters responsible, happily believing that anonymity would save him from discovery. He was summoned to appear before a thoughtful Dr. Welldon. "I have observed," said that venerable gentleman, "certain articles in the *Harrovian* newspaper lately not calculated to increase the respect of the boys for the constituted authorities. As articles in the *Harrovian* are anonymous I shall not dream of inquiring who wrote them. But if any more of the same character appear it may be my painful duty to swish you."

If he escaped this swishing his arrogance let him in for many another. Psychologically he was totally unequipped for the servitude of "fagging," that—to non-English eyes—most inhuman of English school institutions. Fags had to run errands, make teas, clean the boots and do general menial jobs for senior boys who had the authority to punish, and lacking the balance of years, swished harder than the masters. Winston fagged for Nugent Hicks (later the Bishop of Lincoln). After one swishing, received in resentful silence, Winston said cheekily, "I shall be a greater man than you."

"You can have two more for that," said Hicks.

But nothing could stop this incorrigible boy. In one misguided moment of exuberance Winston expertly propelled with his foot a small—deceptively small—boy into the swimming pool; as his victim emerged gasping and furious Winston found to his horror that it was none other than Leo Amery, head of the House, the gym champion and a luminary of the football field. Amery hurled himself on the now deprecating Winston. "I am so sorry," said Winston effusively. "I mistook you for a fourth form boy. You are so small. Ouch! My-father-who-is-a-great-man-is-also-small." Amery laughed and let him go.

When he could, young Winston would find a corner and curl up with one of the fashionable adventure writers of the time. He particularly loved Rider Haggard, who was scarcely thirty years old then, as colorful as his own heroes and the idol of English boyhood. One day with his father Winston met the dashing author himself and was thrilled to receive an autographed copy of *Allen Quarter-main*. Winston wrote dutifully to thank him. "I like 'A.Q.' better than 'King Solomon's Mines'," he wrote. "It is more amusing. I hope you will write a good many more books."

These were the happier memories, but altogether Winston could declare in retrospect, "It is not pleasant to feel oneself so completely outclassed and left behind at the very beginning of the race. . . . I am all for the Public Schools but I don't want to go there again."

To make matters still more heartbreaking for the boy, his father ruined himself politically. His career had flashed too brightly while he was still too young for sound judgment. He had been made Secretary of State for India in 1885, Chancellor of the Exchequer in 1886. Faced with conflicts in the Cabinet, he resigned three times in two years—which proved to be once too often. The third time, probably to his own surprise, his resignation was accepted and Randolph was dispatched to the wilderness, still a favorite of the populace for his vivid and stinging speeches, but his political career ended.

Lady Randolph commented with open bitterness, "The toadies and sycophants fell away and vanished." Randolph went on living in declining health for another nine years, "the chief mourner at his own protracted funeral," as one of his contemporaries remarked, sublimating himself in traveling from the United Kingdom to distant parts of the world, accompanied by his wife.

"It was gall and wormwood to me," Lady Randolph said, "to hear Randolph abused in every quarter, often, as I thought, by the very men who owed their success if not their political existences to him." Gall and wormwood as it was to Lady Randolph, it must have been infinitely worse for Winston, a schoolboy who took the harsh blows of his father's misfortune with full force, unfortified by age or experience. To complete his sense of loss, his American grandfather, Leonard Jerome, died. He had met the old man many times and liked him greatly. Jerome was worried about his grandson of whom all reports were bad, and he had little consolation to take with him

Winston with his mother and his younger brother, John.

to his grave. "He seems backward except for complicated games with soldiers," Jerome was told. And again, "It is difficult to tell what goes on in his mind."

"Let him be," Jerome pleaded. "Boys get good at what they find they shine at." But it was in anxiety for the lad that he died. A big public school, draughty with learning, is not the place for a youth to assimilate such tragedies. Winston became even more withdrawn, but his love of reading and of words was growing greater, and at this period he was said to be able to recite more than a thousand lines of *Lays of Ancient Rome* even when he was reposing at the bottom of the class.

Historic battles and the Army were his chief loves, Marlborough his hero, and he had a fine collection of toy soldiers. His father saw them one day on parade, and putting aside for a moment his preoccupation with his own woes, asked Winston whether he would care to join the Army. "Yes," Winston declared promptly. Here too misfortune stepped in to delay him still further. Playing with his brother Jack in the gardens of Lady Wimbourne's house in Bournemouth, he swung through the branches of a tree, missed his grasp and fell thirty feet. He regained consciousness three days later. For three months he was bedridden, and "for a year," he said, "I looked at life around a corner."

Eventually he recovered sufficiently to study for the entrance examinations to Sandhurst Royal Military Academy. He managed to pass by a squeak at the third attempt after months of cramming and was enrolled in the Awkward Squad for cadets who needed to be brought up to scratch. Sandhurst is not old by British standards, or much storied. English affection is centered almost exclusively on the Royal Navy and has little left over for the Army, which is strange because the English have always been warlike and usually victorious at arms. Actually the Royal Military Academy itself was founded in the same month as the United States Military Academy at West Point, in March, 1802. It is set in the green Berkshire moors and woods, ideal countryside for patriotic and military youth, for it is England at her most béautiful.

Winston was delighted and, happily, before he departed the one heavy cloud on his mind was lifted in a most dramatic and moving way. Winston had never been close to his father. Any clumsy word or move made by the youth to bridge the gap would immediately freeze Randolph in distaste. There is no doubt that the father was disappointed in the son. The first Lord Birkenhead tells in one of his books of a letter, never published, from Lord Randolph to an influential friend in South Africa asking whether an opening could be found for Winston there as there seemed no hope of his making a career for himself in England.

Lord Randolph had been devoting some of the months he spent every year in England to improving his stable of horses, and his mare, the Abbesse de Jouarre, actually won the Oaks in 1889. He took a house for the racing season at Newmarket and it was here

27

by chance that father and son encountered each other, Lord Randolph having been startled by Winston's taking a potshot at a rabbit. They talked of life, of the Army and of the future as they had never talked before. At the end Randolph, made haggard by the approach of death, laid his soul bare in a statement perhaps as heartrending as a father ever made to a son. "Do remember," he said, "things do not always go right with me. My every action is misjudged and every word distorted. . . . So make some allowance."

Never before had Randolph spoken so intimately with his son and never would he do so again. But it transformed the young cadet. What had seemed an impossible dream, some prospect that he might reach a relationship of trust and even friendship with his strange and unhappy father, became feasible. At the same time his mother, pausing in her brilliant round, realized that Winston had reached an age where he could use any influence in Court and society that she could get for him. She spoke to politicians about him, to generals, and even to the Prince of Wales, who invited him to a lunch (at which Winston arrived late). It seemed to Winston all at once that the whole rhythm of his life had changed. Always an able horseman, he found he excelled at the military maneuvers. He cultivated his polo and spent his small allowance on polo ponies. He loved the life. "If only it had been a hundred years earlier," he mused, "what spendid times we should have had! Fancy being nineteen in 1793 with more than twenty years of war against Napoleon in front of one."

Weekends the cadets would descend on London for a rowdy night at the music halls capped with supper at the Café Royal, or the new favorite refuge of the noisier and sportier set, Romano's in the Strand. After two years Winston graduated eighth in a class of 150, a phenomenal leap from the cellar he had so long inhabited.

Now that he was commissioned and projected into the world the door of society opened for him. Lady Randolph saw to that. Lord Randolph died in 1895, a comparatively poor man and what could

Sandhurst. Winston is at left.

Daily Herald of London.

British Information Serv

Lieutenant Churchill of the 4th Hussars.

not be provided was the large fortune needed for him to play his part in that luxurious parade of England in the 1890's. For the whole fall and most of the winter the young officers were in the habit of taking off on a protracted leave in the hunting fields. Winston had neither the urge nor the cash for this. He found his career too exhilarating to set aside for so long. In Cuba where Spain was clinging to one of its remaining footholds in the Americas, there was a rebellion. It wasn't much, but it was enough. Winston gathered what money he had, and, with the permission of the Army authorities, took off for New York and Havana as an observer. On his twenty-first birthday, November 30, 1895, a rebel fired a volley of shots in his general direction and possibly even at him. The Spaniards decorated him and he returned to London in excellent spirits, with a taste for cigars that stayed with him for the rest of his life. With a forbearance he was rarely to show again, he refrained from writing a book about his Cuban adventure.

In the fall of the following year Winston's regiment, the Fourth Hussars, was posted to Bangalore in India. He fitted smoothly into the exotic life of the British officer of the Indian Army, his pay supplemented by an allowance from his family of £500 a year, with batmen and servants and a social life revolving around the polo field. Winston, who had begun by being good at nothing, was now good at everything. He excelled at polo, and he was attracting a lot of attention as a subaltern. He was excited now by appetites some of which he had felt already and some of which were new to him. He wanted to hear the sound of gunfire again and agitated with generals to be allowed to accompany any campaign that might arise. He hungered for the books that he had neglected at school. His afternoon siesta was spent in uninterrupted reading—Plato, Aristotle, Winwood Reade, and, above all, Gibbon. He found he could write and write well, and with his mother representing him enthusiastically in London, he sent off dispatches to the *London Daily Telegraph,* which paid him £5 for the privilege.

In 1897, while he was on leave in London enjoying the season's delights, he read in the press of trouble on the northwest frontier in India. The British general in command in the area was Sir Bindon Blood, whom Winston knew socially and who had actually promised him a chance of active service. He cabled the general and set off at once back to India. Sir Bindon agreed to accept him as a correspondent and Winston found himself in the Khyber Pass, where he was immediately ambushed by Pathans and bore himself with sufficient distinction to be mentioned in dispatches.

Back at his station in Bangalore he wrote not only *The Story of the Malakand Field Force* but also a novel, *Savrola,* which was still vivid enough, even if only as a curiosity, to be serialized recently by a London Sunday newspaper. With this rush of words Winston broke for the first time into serious writing, and there was no doubt about it, he wrote very well indeed. *The Story of the Malakand Field Force* was based on his dispatches to the *Daily Telegraph,* a bright and lively account of frontier campaigning in the course of which he did not hesitate to criticize certain aspects of British military tactics. This annoyed several generals who felt that young subalterns of twenty-three should be seen and not read. But the book pleased the Prime Minister, Lord Salisbury, who chuckled over it, and delighted the Prince of Wales. It is probable that the Prince still felt twinges of regret for his long feud with Lord Randolph, and he followed Winston's activities with unflagging interest. After reading *The Malakand Field Force* he wrote Winston a remarkable fan letter.

"My dear Winston," the letter began. "I cannot resist writing a few lines to congratulate you on the success of your book! I have read it with the greatest possible interest and I think the descriptions and the language generally excellent. Everybody is reading it, and I only hear it spoken of with praise. Having now seen active service you will wish to see more, and have a great chance I am sure of winning the V.C. . . ."

MAJOR-GENERAL SIR BINDON BLOOD, K.C.B., COMMANDING MALAKAND
FIELD FORCE.

THE STORY

OF THE

MALAKAND FIELD FORCE

AN EPISODE OF FRONTIER WAR

BY

WINSTON L. SPENCER CHURCHILL
Lieutenant, the 4th Queen's Own Hussars

"They (Frontier Wars) are but the surf that marks the edge and
the advance of the wave of civilisation."
LORD SALISBURY, Guildhall, 1892

WITH MAPS, PLANS, ETC.

LONGMANS, GREEN, AND CO.
39 PATERNOSTER ROW, LONDON
NEW YORK AND BOMBAY
1898

But Winston had cause to regret *The Story of the Malakand Field Force.* The biggest British force in years was building up in Egypt to invade the Sudan under General Sir Herbert Kitchener. This force was to advance up the Nile to the Sudan, attack the Khalifah's Dervishes and avenge the death of General Gordon, whose murder had hung over British military pride ever since Khartoum had fallen to the Mahdi thirteen years earlier in 1885. Every officer in the British Army clamored to be included in the expedition, Winston Churchill among them. Unfortunately for him, Kitchener had read *The Story of the Malakand Field Force* and had expressed his views to intimates on what he thought of cheeky young subalterns who told generals how to fight campaigns. He refused pointblank to have Winston Churchill in his expedition even after Lord Salisbury, the Prime Minister, had been persuaded by Lady Randolph to use his influence personally. It became a battle of wills between England's

General Sir Herbert Kitchener.

unbeatable and most distinguished soldier and the twenty-four-year-old Lieutenant Winston Churchill. Winston won. Realizing that he could never get to the campaign as a soldier, he requested leave of absence from his regiment and went out as a war correspondent, at his own expense and with no responsibility to the Crown.

The line between the correspondent and the soldier was not one which Winston Churchill has ever been able to draw precisely. He had already written in *The Story of the Malakand Field Force* that "I can never doubt which is the right end to be at. It is better to be making the news than taking it; to be an actor rather than a critic." As Kitchener's army advanced into the Sudan and prepared to do battle before Omdurman, Winston would have been best advised to stay close to the telegraph and wireless facilities. But instead he attached himself to the Twenty-first Cavalry, which was being held as a shock unit. This was complicated because he had dislocated his shoulder and had his arm strapped to his side. Secondly, as a correspondent, he should not have borne weapons, an offense which, should he be taken prisoner, would deny him the rights a prisoner may expect from a chivalrous enemy. Winston was armed with sword and pistol. He was on reconnaissance near Omdurman when he saw a great army of Dervishes, on horse and on foot, with banners in gorgeous array, begin to advance. "Talk of fun," cried Churchill in retrospect. "Where will you beat this! On horseback, at daybreak, within shot of an advancing army, seeing everything. . . ." The Dervishes rode with fierce hopelessness into the full flame of disciplined British infantry and artillery fire. The three hundred horsemen of the Twenty-first Cavalry wheeled to the trumpet's order into line, leveled lances and charged into a pack of several thousand barefooted riflemen. It was all over in three minutes, the most brilliant cavalry action since the Charge of the Light Brigade. A quarter of the British force was lost at once and 120 of their horses fell. The British were swallowed up, hacking and firing into the mass. Winston found himself alone fighting off spears, shot several Dervishes dead and fought his way back to the British lines.

Elated at still being alive, he hailed a sergeant of the Lancers. "Well," he cried, "how did you enjoy yourself?"

"I don't say I exactly enjoyed it, sir," said the sergeant, "but I think I'll get more used to it next time."

The charge itself had not achieved much, but the Dervish force as a whole stood no chance against the trained soldiers and were all but annihilated. The war was won and Gordon avenged.

Within a week Winston was on his way back to England, planning in his mind the book which he would write about the Nile campaign. He was now a figure in his own right in England as a successful journalist and well-known soldier. But four years in the Army had tied him in knots in his attempt to balance his budget. He spent lavishly when he had it, and also when he had not. He bought polo ponies, traveled, dined well. Clearly he could make more money as a writer, and still see military action, than he could in the service of the Queen, where he was at the mercy of the Kitcheners and Bloods who might at any time stop him from participating in the adventure that he loved.

He resolved to resign his commission, but first he returned to India to help the Fourth Hussars win the interregimental polo tournament. Some days before the game he slipped on some stairs and dislocated his arm, but managed to play with his elbow strapped to his side, preventing him from hitting hard. Still the Fourth Hussars won and went in to the final play-off. Churchill, his elbow in place again, hit two goals and the tournament was won.

On the way back to London he buried himself in his cabin to write *The River War*, which for a young man of twenty-four was a masterpiece of fast-moving narrative, containing one of the most vivid accounts ever written of a cavalry charge. "I hope," he wrote prophetically at one point, "that if evil days should come upon our country, and the last army which a collapsing Empire could interpose between London and the invader were dissolving in rack and ruin, there would be some, even in these modern days, who would

36

With the Hussars in Bangalore.

not care to accustom themselves to a new order of things and tamely survive disaster."

And in one inspired sentence the whole atmosphere of a military camp on the eve of battle is caught. "The Lancers lay down to sleep and thanked heaven they were not Generals and had nothing but their lives to lose."

It was exciting, it was heady, and the money coming in opened the way to still another career that had been in his mind for some time, politics. This he could never have pursued if he had remained in the Army. Members of Parliament were unpaid and needed their own fortunes to support themselves. Winston, by his birth and family, would automatically have entered politics but he was determined to accept no money from his widowed mother. Journalism was providing money even though it seemed a dubious and impermanent way of making a living. Winston persuaded Conservative Central Office to let him stand at a special election in Oldham, Lancashire. No residence qualifications were necessary then, or are now, in English politics, and while the system results sometimes in a rather desultory association between the Member and his constituents it enables a political party to spread its talent evenly through the country and to its best advantage. Oldham was strongly Liberal but it was felt that the campaign would give Winston some necessary political blooding. This was an age of two-member seats so that Winston fought side by side with a Tory of working-class origin, which led to their being dubbed, "the Scion and the Socialist," but they made little impact and the Liberals won comfortably.

That ended politics for the time being. In South Africa the Boer War had broken out. Winston took a cab to Fleet Street and called in at the office of the *Morning Post,* emerging with a contract. His salary was to be £250 a month, plus expenses, a sum which only a handful of journalists in Fleet Street earn to this day. He was twenty-four years old.

Part II

The Storm Gathers

Winston in South Africa.

2

The Storm Gathers

"Oh, break the news to muvver,
And tell 'er 'ow I love 'er,
And kiss 'er dear sweet lips for me
'Cos I ain't coming 'ome."

WITH THAT NOTABLY UN-MARTIAL SONG THE BRITISH ARMY LANDED at Cape Town, exercised its horses, and prepared to ride on Pretoria, capital of the Boers. There seemed to be nothing much in the way to stop them. It was October of 1899. On the high seas, bound from Southampton to South Africa, without wireless or news, Winston fretted the days away in an agony of seasickness and apprehension. It was inconceivable that the Boers, a rabble of farmers, would still be in the field when the ship arrived.

Ahead of Winston a letter was on the way to Lord Milner, the South African High Commissioner, from Joe Chamberlain, the Colonial Secretary, and it told of Winston's coming. "He is a very clever young fellow," Chamberlain wrote, "with many of his father's qualifications. He has the reputation for being bumptious, but I have not myself found him so, and time will no doubt get rid of the defect if he has it. . . . He is a good writer and full of energy. He hopes to be in Parliament, but want of means stands in his way."

Meanwhile the war was not going as expected. In the veldt the British were learning that fast-riding, dedicated crack-shot settlers who knew and hungered for the land had immense advantages over

41

soldiers in red who fought by the book. By the time Winston arrived the Boer ponies from the Transvaal and the Orange Free State were trotting confidently through the British province of Natal. Mafeking was surrounded by Boer commandoes, and so was Kimberley where Cecil Rhodes, the great visionary of imperialism in South Africa, was living. Worse still, the Transvaalers had cut the railroad from Glencoe to Ladysmith, and Free Staters descending from the Drakensberg plateau bordering the Orange Free State and Basutoland pressed on Ladysmith, the British center of operations. Before the bewildered Imperial forces knew what was happening they were bottled up inside the city. A last-ditch effort to prevent the junction of the two enveloping wings was beaten by the Boer General de Wet whose mixed force killed and captured 1,500 British soldiers at Lombard's Kop and completed the encirclement of the city. Through these first months disaster and defeat occupied the news dispatches almost without relief, and Britain, who had budgeted for a quick colonial action, had to prepare instead for a full-scale war against a determined and astute enemy, well generaled and fanatical.

Winston moved with the troops as close to the Ladysmith area as the Boer forces would allow. His assignment was to accompany an armored train manned by Irish soldiers, which was seeking to harry the besieging burghers. He pitched a tent with his old schoolmate, Leo Amery, who was covering the war for the *London Times*. Amery was leather-tough, wrinkled even as a youth, and aggressive. He had climbed some of the sheerest peaks of the world and his air of fierceness was all the greater for his being such a little fellow. He and Winston were good friends now and their pleasure in each other's company was made all the sharper by the little needles of rivalry they kept jabbing into each other.

One wet morning they were awakened as usual by their batman who told them that the train was ready to make its sortie. Amery mumbled into his sleeping bag. The train, he declared, had never left on time yet and he saw no reason for presuming it would today, after which he went to sleep again. Winston, however, crawling out to shave, saw that the train had steam up and that the Irish and Durban soldiers who manned it were already aboard. He had only a few seconds in which to decide. If he waited for Amery he would miss the operation, so, shamelessly abandoning his friend, he raced for the train. Amery heard it move and sat up raging. Now, an armored train may have had its uses against some of the primitive enemies Imperial soldiers had fought in the past, but against the Boers it was a cumbersome and dubious weapon. On this occasion a Boer ambush watched it pass near Estcourt and then blew up the line, an obvious move. Into the confusion the Boers then turned three hundred rifles, two pieces of artillery and a pom-pom gun. It was murder. Winston, at the first volley exchanging, as he put it, "the comparative peace and safety of a railway accident for the firing line," hit the dirt. So furious was the Boer fire that the Irish troops were able to reply only sporadically. This was not Winston Churchill's kind of war. He made his way cautiously to the engine where the driver was tending his wounds and was, as Winston noted with approval, in good spirits. With the help of some of the soldiers they managed to get the train back onto the rails, Winston giving the orders from an exposed knoll and shouting above the fire. Others fell; Winston remained on his feet.

Only the engine and the tender could be moved. The rest of the train had to be abandoned to the enemy. Forty of the most seriously wounded were piled into the tender. Walking wounded were ordered to hang on, and the unwounded to run after it. The Boer fire did not slacken and each shell burst added to the casualties. With Winston directing from the locomotive, the desperate cortege moved off, and at once there was chaos. Wounded men fell screaming from the sides of a tender made slippery with blood. Slowly as the train moved, it was leaving behind men still caught in the gauntlet of flying bullets, and shouting for help.

Winston could not leave them at the mercy of the enemy. He

General Louis Botha.

leaped from the moving train to assist the stranded men on foot who had passed out of sight. Before he knew it he was alone on the track with Boer infantrymen descending on him. He threw himself down against a storm of bullets. On his feet again, pursued by soldiers, he made like a hare for the protection of a bank. A Boer horseman charged him; Churchill reached for his gun to drop the man and realized he had left it behind him on the train.

"Surrender!" A face of unusual humor, with slanted oriental eyes, grinned down at him. It was perhaps as well that Churchill was without his gun, because his captor was Louis Botha, one of the best marksmen in the Boer Army (and subsequently South Africa's first Prime Minister). The sound of the fighting had died now. The remnants of the stranded force had thrown down their arms and been taken prisoner. Fading away in the distance the locomotive and tender whistled its relief and deliverance. Churchill was alone among the Boers. He realized for the first time that he was slightly wounded in the hand.

Nothing in the world is such a shock to a proud and adventurous man as to find himself unexpectedly made a prisoner of war. The next few hours were a nightmare. The rain fell and without food he was marched through the grasslands to the burghers' headquarters. His morale might have been a little higher had he known that that same night a letter was mailed to the general manager of the Natal Railways from the inspector stating that "the railwaymen who accompanied the armored train this morning . . . convey their admiration of the coolness and pluck displayed by Winston Churchill, the war correspondent . . . to whose efforts backed up by the driver, Wagner, is due the fact that the armored engine and tender were brought successfully out. . . . The whole of our men are loud in their praise of Mr. Churchill who, I regret to say, is a prisoner. I respectfully ask you to convey their admiration to a brave man."

Churchill's identity was soon established, and the Boers hailed the capture of a prisoner of major importance. It was a depressing experience. The first few weeks of prison life are always the worst. After that a soldier makes his peace with captivity. Churchill roamed the prison camp in Pretoria like a bear, conjuring up and then dismissing scheme after scheme for escape. One of his plans was a coup to storm and take over the prison itself. Finally he planned a breakout over an ill-guarded wall with two officers, one of whom happily spoke Afrikaans. The trip to the safety of Portuguese East Africa was three hundred miles, and in addition to a compass and maps they had chocolates and some concentrated meat. Once action had been agreed upon Churchill felt better. The Churchill *joie de vivre* returned. He paid his mess bills, cashed a check for £20, and wrote with extravagant politeness a good-by letter to the Boer Minister of War in Pretoria. As a finishing touch he stole, for disguise, a Dutch pastor's hat which was not strictly necessary, consorted not at all with his uniform, and can only be really explained as the beginning of a subsequently celebrated and apparently uncontrollable urge toward sartorial eccentricity.

From the hiding place of a lavatory the escape began. Churchill, first as usual, scaled the wall and disappeared into the brush while he waited for the others. There was the sound of frenzied movement on the other side, whispered warnings that guards were approaching. The game was up. The escape was off. What was Churchill to do? He was alone on the outside, without the maps or the compass, only the chocolates. The temptation to scurry back into the uncomfortable but secure haven of the camp must have been strong, but it was impossible for him mentally to unscrew himself from his tension of resolve. He probably guessed that if he went back now he would never make another break. He emerged from the brush, dusted himself, set his pastor's hat at an angle and strolled nonchalantly into the brightly lit streets of enemy Pretoria, hearing on all sides a strange staccato language not a word of which he knew. If anyone accosted him he was lost.

Nevertheless his spirits soared. The dead weight of the prison camp had dropped from him. He made his way to the railroad station and leaped aboard a freight train. He did not know where it was going, but he hoped it was in the direction of Portuguese East Africa. Whichever direction it was heading, however, it would take him away from the prison camp.

He was unaware of the furore his escape had aroused in Pretoria when it was discovered. The houses of British citizens in the capital were searched and ransacked, sandy-topped suspects hauled in, walloped and released. A somewhat petulant description of Winston was circulated. "Englishman, 25 years old, about five feet eight inches tall, indifferent build, walks with a forward stoop, pale appearance, red-brownish hair, small and hardly noticeable moustache, talks through his nose and cannot pronounce the letter S correctly." A reward of £25 was offered for his arrest dead or alive, a sum hardly in keeping with the importance of the prisoner but explained by the fact that the head jailer would have to pay it out of his own pocket.

Meanwhile Winston was not faring well. Moved by a logic that could only come to a man so hard-pressed, he jumped off the train before dawn and continued on foot so that he could acquire intelligence concerning his whereabouts. Making his way painfully through high grass and swamp under an inhuman sun, he became conscious of his weakness due to confinement and malnutrition. As the hours passed his feet became heavier and his exhaustion became near-delirium. Finding himself in a small community at nightfall, he realized he had to seek help at whatever cost or danger. Someone passed in the darkness and Winston called out to him. By a stroke of the most unbelievable luck the man proved to be an Englishman, the only Englishman in hundreds of miles. Winston, as he was led off to a hasty sanctuary, was told that had he spoken to another human being he would have been arrested, as the whole country was on the lookout for him. He was then left at the bottom of a mine with some food, candles and a copy of Robert Louis Stevenson's *Kidnapped* until means of transportation could be devised.

Three days later he was smuggled aboard a train bound for Laurenço Marques in Portuguese East Africa. Once more one is startled by the calculated recklessness of this young man. He had accepted from his benefactor a pistol for emergency. Recaptured unarmed he would almost certainly have been returned to camp little the worse for his adventure, for the Boers were not brutes. Caught with a firearm there is little doubt that he would have faced an instant firing squad. Fortunately he did not use the pistol until he passed the customs check on the Portuguese border. Then, realizing he was safe, he fired several volleys into the air from sheer joy. Arriving in Laurenço Marques he hurried to the British consulate, as black as a chimney sweep. The Consul, after the first disconcerting moment of being presented to this wild, grinning creature, gave a yell heard round the British Empire. Winston Churchill had escaped!

Returning to Durban he received a hero's welcome from the townspeople and from all the ships in the harbor blowing their sirens and flying their bunting. The war had continued to go badly in Winston's unwilling absence, and he emerged as the one piece of good news that England had received. He was, at this point, his country's first hero. He was asked to make speeches and he enthusiastically complied, dampening the chauvinists by his tributes to a "dignified and honorable enemy." After that he headed back to the fighting. He was eager to be a soldier again and once more

48

Winston Churchill speaking at Durban after his escape.

HOW I ESCAPED
FROM PRETORIA.

By Winston Churchill.

THE *Morning Post* has received the following telegram from Mr. Winston Spencer Churchill, its war correspondent, who was taken prisoner by the Boers and escaped from Pretoria.

LOURENCO MARQUES, December 21st, 10 p.m.

I was concealed in a railway truck under great sacks.

I had a small store of good water with me.

I remained hidden, chancing discovery.

The Boers searched the train at Komati Poort, but did not search deep enough, so after sixty hours of misery I came safely here.

I am very weak, but I am free.

I have lost many pounds weight, but I am lighter in heart.

I shall also avail myself of every opportunity from this moment to urge with earnestness an unflinching and uncompromising prosecution of the war.

On the afternoon of the 12th the Transvaal Government's Secretary for War informed me that there was little chance of my release.

I therefore resolved to escape the same night, and left the State Schools Prison at Pretoria by climbing the wall when the sentries' backs were turned momentarily.

I walked through the streets of the town without any disguise, meeting many burghers, but I was not challenged in the crowd.

I got through the pickets of the Town Guard, and struck the Delagoa Bay Railroad.

I walked along it, evading the watchers at the bridges and culverts.

I waited for a train beyond the first station.

The out 11.10 goods train from Pretoria arrived, and before it had reached full speed I boarded with great difficulty, and hid myself under coal sacks.

I jumped from the train before dawn, and sheltered during the day in a small wood, in company with a huge vulture, who displayed a lively interest in me.

I walked on at dusk.

There were no more trains that night.

The danger of meeting the guards of the railway line continued; but I was obliged to follow it, as I had no compass or map.

I had to make wide *détours* to avoid the bridges, stations, and huts.

My progress was very slow, and chocolate is not a satisfying food.

The outlook was gloomy, but I persevered, with God's help, for five days.

The food I had to have was very precarious.

I was lying up at daylight, and walking on at night time, and, meanwhile, my escape had been discovered and my description telegraphed everywhere.

All the trains were searched.

Everyone was on the watch for me.

Four wrong people were arrested.

But on the sixth day I managed to board a train beyond Middleburg, whence there is a direct service to Delagoa.

took the Queen's commission as a lieutenant in a somewhat nondescript outfit called the South African Light Horse. The attraction of this regiment for Winston can only be explained by its uniform which included a huge, plumed floppy hat.

Meanwhile the war was taking a turn for the better as the Boers began to give before the superior organization and strength of the British. The siege of Ladysmith was lifted in February, 1900, and Winston was in one of the first squadrons riding into the city. Not long afterward he was almost taken prisoner again. His horse fell and bolted, leaving Winston stranded in the open veldt and with bullets flying. He started to run for it, leaped behind a mounted fellow officer and they made their way out together. Remembering that the Boer Minister of War had in his possession a letter of good-by from Winston before he escaped from the prisoner-of-war camp, one can imagine that a second meeting would have been a warm one.

The Boers were on the run now. The Boer President, Kruger, was in full flight from Pretoria, his capital, and the British again thought—again wrongly—that the war was all but over. Winston

Lieutenant Churchill of the South African Light Horse.

rode with Field Marshal Lord Roberts's victorious armies first into Johannesburg, and then into Pretoria. He was wildly received at the prison camp from which he had escaped almost a year earlier. The Boers scattered and settled down grimly to a guerrilla warfare which was to last another two years.

Winston returned to England and another hero's reception. It is hard to realize, in contemplating the scenes of enthusiasm greeting this hard-bitten veteran fighting man and accomplished journalist, that only eight years had passed since a resentful, delicate, unhappy misfit had entered Sandhurst by the skin of his teeth.

Winston had left England in the nineteenth century and he returned to it in the twentieth, twenty-six years old and the most famous young man in England. Queen Victoria was not yet laid to rest but Britain was shifting subtly from the Victorian to the Edwardian age, to what would be remembered as the last age of mature pleasure in our world's history. England was still confident of her supremacy in the world but she was aware of new problems demanding more complicated solutions than old principles could provide. Socialism and the trades union movement had emerged but had not yet settled on their political direction. Motor cars had arrived and airplanes were on the way. The Victorian seeds had flowered. From Dean Street Soho, where Karl Marx had brought to working class philosophy a diabolical new impetus, to the cricket field where Dr. W. G. Grace had blasted the old English "play-the-game" ideal to smithereens with the noise of his bat and his rage to win, the old standards were crumbling.

But the institutions were still strong. Politics remained a noble profession and politicians were esteemed as they never were in the United States or in France. Suffragettes were beginning to quack and clack on the sidelines doing their best to bring statesmanship down to their level, and the handful of Irish nationalist M.P.s in the House were always eager for hooliganism. Nevertheless politics in Westminster in the first fourteen years of the century reached a level

Vanity Fair, from the collection of The Old Print Seller.
The author of *Savrola* in 1900.

of intelligence, wit and dignity that has never been equaled since and is unlikely to be equaled again.

Flushed by apparent victory in South Africa, the Conservatives had called a snap election—which was their constitutional right— two years before their term of office expired, hoping to take advantage of their popularity, and Winston was determined to take part in it. He had fought his first election more or less as an apprentice. This time the constituencies were shouldering and butting each other in the rush to have the young hero for candidate. He could have accepted the easiest offer and ridden into Westminster on a safe seat, but he would not have been Winston Churchill. He elected to return to Oldham and fight it out again in the strongly Liberal constituency which had already rejected him. There he had a hard fight and won by only 222 votes.

With his political career launched and a few months to go before he took his seat, he concentrated on his most important problem, making money. His expenses were high. Until comparatively recent years Churchill always needed to make big money to keep up with the standard of living he insisted on, being, as a friend remarked, "easily satisfied with the best."

In the months available to him Winston went—successfully—after the jackpot. The South African War had already yielded a stream of newspaper articles. He now delivered himself of two books on the campaign and his part in it, accepted the offer of a lecture tour in England followed by a lecture tour in the United States. As a speaker he was learning fast. When Irishmen tried to heckle him in America he smoothly switched to the accomplishments and courage of the Irish troops in South Africa and was greeted with thunderous cheers.

This burst of activity earned him nearly £15,000 at a time when the pound was worth five dollars, and a pound was a pound and the dollar a dollar and income tax was a shilling on the pound. Winston was suddenly a rich young man and spending it as fast as he made it.

New York 1900.

He never had any compunction about the large sums he earned or the purpose for which he wanted it. Years later Leo Amery was still somewhat annoyed at being left in a tent in South Africa and made some comment about early birds getting caught. "True," acknowledged Winston with immense complacency. "But if I had not been caught I would not have escaped, and my imprisonment and escape provided me with the materials for lectures and a book which brought me in enough money to get into Parliament," adding unkindly, "ten years before you did."

On February 18, 1901, Winston rose in the House for the first time. It is an admirable tradition of the House, studiously observed, that a new Member is heard with courtesy and attention when he makes his maiden speech. This is the moment when old Members assess Parliamentary timber and material for future office. But though they listen with respect they miss nothing, and a bad maiden speech can result in the Member receiving a very uncomfortable time when he rises again. Disraeli, for example, made a notably bad maiden speech, and this, together with his extravagant taste in clothes and his histrionic style, aroused all the bad manners of which some Members are capable, and for a long time thereafter he could rarely rise without being greeted with a catcall from some corner of the House. How many young Members have made their maiden speeches, flattered by this initial politeness into dreaming of future glory, only to find next time that Members walk out, go to sleep or chatter among themselves! Many hopes die between the first and second speeches in the House of Commons.

A maiden speech by Winston Churchill, the gallant son of a famous father, a national hero, an acknowledged and successful public speaker, was something special even by the standards of the House. Winston had rehearsed his speech carefully. It was commendably short and dealt with the conduct of the still-dragging war in South Africa. He paid tribute to the martial skill of the Boers "who are fighting in the field," and he added aggressively, "If I were a Boer I hope I should be fighting in the field" (a remark which, as Joe Chamberlain said cynically to a neighbor, was "a good way to throw away seats"). He finished with a nice tribute to his father, thanking the House for its kindness and patience, "which have been extended to me, I well know, not on my account, but because of a certain splendid memory which many honorable members still preserve."

Afterward there were the usual tributes to a good start by various veterans of the House, but they could not be called immoderate in their praise. Some of his remarks smacked of the "Tory democracy" his father had preached and made Conservatives feel uncomfortable. The Liberals were intrigued. Listening with more care than most to the speech was the tremendous little Welshman, David Lloyd George, eleven years Winston's senior and already the most brilliant

56

The "terrible twins"; David Lloyd George and Winston Churchill.

of a brilliant assembly. No one could remain unshaken by the violence of Lloyd George's rhetoric directed against the Conservatives, for whom he had an instinctive contempt, detestation even. Lloyd George had been in the House since 1890 but as the Liberals had been the minority party almost without a break since 1886 he had known no office, a situation which creates frustration among ambitious politicians while it sharpens their teeth. Introduced to Winston, Lloyd George told him admiringly in a fine phrase, "You are standing against the light." A memorable if chequered friendship was taking shape.

The next three years saw a curious change in Winston's career. For one thing, the journalist became a historian. His two-volume biography of Lord Randolph Churchill appeared and some critics still consider it the best thing he has ever done. But while his literary reputation soared his political career seemed to be heading for a violent end.

Joseph Chamberlain.

His personal power drive was of such impetus that his reflexes, reactions, impressions were quickened to lightning pitch, as though he were in a race with life. Above all he seemed to have an extra sensitivity for anything that touched upon his father and his father's record. There were many who remembered Lord Randolph, some with dislike, some with a twinge of conscience. Winston seemed to seek them out to vent his resentment on them. Then again some of the younger Members were patently jealous of Winston's seething talents. Every House of Commons, no matter how excellent, has its quota of pests. These pests had noticed with derision at Winston's first speech that he found it difficult to pronounce the letter S. Consequently every time he rose to speak he would hear hissing noises from usually untraceable corners of the Chamber, too faint for the Speaker to detect, but on Winston and his speeches the noises had a disconcerting effect.

Lastly but most importantly of all, there was the political direction of the Conservative Government under Arthur Balfour which was taking, for Winston, a most alarming course. On the traditional English dispute between free trade and protection Winston was, as his father had been, an instinctive believer in *laissez-faire* and free trade. But under the influence of Joe Chamberlain, the Colonial Secretary, the Tories were moving steadily in the direction of protection. Chamberlain was a colorful and popular figure in English life with his monocle, his inevitable orchid and his cigar. In his time he had done favors for Winston, and had even come to campaign for him on his last election. But on an issue as fundamental to an English politician as free trade or protection friendship did not count. Outside the House they continued to receive each other jovially in their clubs, but inside the House they were enemies. Winston may also have remembered that Chamberlain had been an old political adversary of his father's.

Anger, then, at Tory policy, suspicion of his father's old enemies, irritation at the nameless nonentities who harried him, were the emotions which suffused the face that Winston Churchill turned to the world, and he sometimes gave the impression of a young man both harsh and cruel. To those who did not know him, according to F. E. Smith, one of his best friends, "he is reserved, insolent and even domineering. . . . He has no small talk; and says everything which comes into his mind. . . . He walks through the lobbies with an air appropriate to Napoleon Bonaparte on the morning of the crisis of the 18th Brumaire." (Smith in the same context added, "There is no man in public life in England with a heart so warm, with a simplicity so complete, with a loyalty so unswerving and dependable.")

Between Winston and the rest of the Tories, cracks appeared. The cracks became a breach, the breach shuddered toward an open break. Brashness was something older Tories with their strong ancestral links could forgive, and they respected filial loyalty even when they themselves received the barbs. They were themselves irritated by Winston's hecklers and many shared his free trade views. But they began to suspect that Winston's views were more radical than conservative. He advocated a just and honorable peace for the Boers. Like his father he attacked the military budget. All this annoyed the die-hards. Then he attacked Chamberlain in his speeches, and even Balfour, the most courteous of prime ministers, was furious. The Tory Party that reassembled after the 1904 recess was in an ugly mood and the anger was directed at Churchill. When he rose to speak he was howled down. Another time when he rose Balfour and his supporters walked out, an act to intimidate the boldest freshman M.P. Winston refused to be silenced. He would not be what he described in his work on Randolph, one of those M.P.s: "a silent drudge, tramping at intervals through lobbies to record his vote, and wondering why he came to Westminster at all."

Then in 1904 his constituency at Oldham disowned him. They could not turn him out, not at least until the next election, but they could leave him a political waif and stray. In May of that year Winston, amid the deafening howls and catcalls of the Tories and the counter-cheers of the Liberals, walked across to the other side

60

The London Electrotype Agency, Ltd.

Young Parliamentarian.

of the Chamber. Lloyd George with alacrity moved across the bench to give Winston space next to him.

Winston was now a Liberal. He had burned his boats and was sitting profile to profile among new and alien colleagues morose from long years in the minority, men he was accustomed to regard full-face from the fat benches of the governing party. There are few precedents in English history for such a change, and most men who have attempted it disappeared quickly and permanently from public life. Winston's fate was strikingly—and from the Tory point of view exasperatingly—different. Two years after his defection the nation went to the polls. The Liberals won by the smashing majority of 401 to 157 and Henry Campbell-Bannerman became Prime Minister. With exquisite pleasure he phialed the necessary drop of wormwood into the Conservatives' cup of gall. He made Winston Under-Secretary for the Colonies. Not only was the renegade sitting there arrogantly on the Government side of the House, he had been given office!

Almost at once his enemies nearly got him. In the course of a debate on South African affairs, Lord Milner, the High Commissioner, was criticized for authorizing the flogging of Chinese laborers in the colony. It was Winston's duty to reply on behalf of the government and he did not enjoy it. He condemned the flogging of coolies but pleaded with the House to refrain from the censure of individuals. He made a poor speech which Balfour, replying, reduced to shreds. The Tories, who had bayed continually at Winston, roared with mirth at Balfour's sallies. It was a bad beating, such as some junior Ministers have taken never to rise again. All it did to Winston was make him determined never to repeat his mistake. All speeches henceforth had to be irreproachable. For the next eight years, perhaps the most strenuous in the history of British politics, he was continually in office and in the forefront of public affairs.

In 1906 he visited Germany to watch the German Army maneuvers. It was a formidable display and an important event in shaping his outlook. Kaiser Wilhelm paid him great attention and went out

With the Kaiser in Germany. Said Churchill, "The defense which can be made of him will not be flattering to his self-esteem . . . Look at him. He is only a blunderer."

of his way to impress the young English statesman. The result was that Winston was uncompromisingly pro-French from that moment.

In 1907 King Edward VII made him a Privy Councillor. In 1908 Campbell-Bannerman resigned and died a month later. He had governed less than three years, but with his death an important personality had passed from the scene. Campbell-Bannerman had granted, in his short period of administration, autonomy to the Orange Free State and the Transvaal. The latter award must surely have been the most magnanimous ever made to a defeated people by their conqueror, but granted as it was only four years after the peace treaty with the memories of English "atrocities" so new in Boer minds, it created no goodwill. An aged peer eulogizing on the late Prime Minister's virtues in the House of Lords, went berserk half way through while praising the devotion of his wife. "All the more commendable," said the peer going pale and swaying, "because (she) was an ugly old b. . . ." After a horrified hubbub it was arranged that *Hansard*, the English record of Parliamentary debate, be expurgated.

Campbell-Bannerman was succeeded by Herbert Asquith and a new phase of England's development began. Asquith took Lloyd George from the Board of Trade and made him Chancellor of the Exchequer, and made Winston President of the Board of Trade (equivalent of America's Secretary of Commerce) with a seat in the Cabinet. In the same year Winston married.

No matter how it is presented in any account of Churchill's life, this last fact always comes as a slight shock. Such is the momentum, the bumpy but non-stop progress of his career, that his private life is not only lost but forgotten. Yet it was a very agreeable private life. Until 1904, at any rate, Winston was one of the country's more eligible bachelors. He shared an apartment at 12 Bolton Street in Mayfair with his brother John, who was on the Stock Ex-

Text within the image: PRIVY COUNCIL·L·, BEACONSFIELD, CHURCHILL

E. T. Reid, Punch.

Privy Councillor at 32.

Young man-about-town.

change, and took delight in the sybaritic pleasures of this splendid decade. He indulged in cigars and had acquired a fondness for wine which later became world famous. Weekends were spent in the country playing polo, which he did superbly well, or golf, which was not so good. After his switch to the Liberals his eligibility dropped somewhat. Tory hostesses resented what they considered his desertion. His ostracism was not so dramatic or as obliterating as that of his father, and he was in demand by Liberal hostesses, but he was widely regarded as a young man too clever by half, and not to be trusted. And in fairness it should be acknowledged he must have been a difficult person for his fellow men to love, moved as he was by his impulses, his open ambition, his recklessness. At thirty-three he was just too successful. What critics are invariably reluctant to admit, however, is that success is nearly always based on hard work and concentration that the critic himself could never hope to match. Winston, even on country-party weekends, took heavy case-loads of notes with him for study.

Women saw him differently. Because his marriage has been such a happy one as to eliminate his private life completely from the Churchill story, the picture of the young Churchill from the woman's point of view has been largely ignored. There can be no doubt however that he was extremely attractive to women. We have this fact not only from the English Queen of Rumania, who may well have sighed for Winston's strength in the years she was married to the inept Prince Ferdinand, but also from Consuelo Vanderbilt, the American heiress who married his cousin, the Duke of Marlborough, and who writes with unabashed admiration: "He struck me as ardent and vital and seemed to have every intention of getting the most out of life, whether in sport, in love, in adventure or in politics."

True, the Dowager Duchess of Marlborough called him "a little upstart," but she was an old woman and worried over the possibility of Consuelo's being unable to produce an heir, in which case Winston would inherit the title.

The Honorable Clementine Hozier.

Even the Fabian Socialist Beatrice Webb, whose head was far too full of reform and revolution ever to think of such things as sex appeal and thought Churchill "restless, egotistical, bumptious, shallow-minded and reactionary," also admitted that he had "a certain personal magnetism, great pluck and some originality—not of intellect but of character."

It is clear that Winston Churchill spent his bachelorhood too deeply immersed in Winston Churchill to notice his fascination for women, and from his writings seems to have been more surprised than anyone else when Clementine Hozier, a gorgeous Scottish girl with beautiful eyes, twenty-three years old, fell in love with him. "Clemmie" was the daughter of Colonel Sir H. M. Hozier of the Third Dragoons, her mother the Countess of Airlie, who liked Winston and said of him, "He is so like Lord Randolph. He has some of his faults and all his qualities. He is gentle and tender, and affectionate to those he loves, much hated by those who have not come under his personal charm."

Winston and Clementine were married at St. Margaret's, Westminster, on September 12, 1908. It was the social event of the year. The comments as the young couple walked down the aisle however were not all flattering. Churchill looked "powerful but ugly" according to a friend of the family, while Lord Rosebery forecast, "It won't last six months." It has now lasted through fifty years of the most shattering disaster and the most lofty triumph in unswerving mutual devotion, and has yielded five children: Diana, born in 1909 ("The prettiest child ever seen," Churchill told Lloyd George. "The very image of me"); Randolph, born in 1911; Sarah, in 1914; Marigold, born in 1918, who died as a child, and Mary, born in 1922.

Meanwhile his career continued skyward, but a few ominous signs were appearing. In 1910, at a time of worsening industrial relations, Winston moved from the Board of Trade to the Home Office (similar to America's Department of the Interior), and in the same year his friend and mentor, King Edward VII, died. One of

Winston's first tasks at the Home Office was to maintain order through an outburst of bitter strikes. Acting with characteristic speed and vigor, he moved troops into the Rhondda and Aberdare Valleys of Wales when violence threatened among striking coal miners, and though the violence did not materialize his act infuriated trade unionists. For the first time "militarist" became a word to be thrown at Winston by Socialists on all occasions. In 1911 there was an unauthorized strike on the North Eastern Railway. In the same year the Sailors' and Firemen's Union struck, followed by the dockers, carters and vanmen. An ominous situation worried the nation's leaders. Then there was another railroad strike and the new King George V, who was not in London, sent a telegram to Winston asking whether he was satisfied that order could be preserved. "The difficulty," Winston replied, "is not to maintain order but to maintain order without loss of life." This message was not made public, so that the workers and strikers had no idea of Winston's overriding anxiety to avoid bloodshed and violence. All they saw was a young and ruthless government official keeping strikes under control with the use of soldiers and special constables. The miners led a hard life and their only luxury was bitterness and a long memory. They would not forget what Winston had done.

In the Commons Winston backed Lloyd George in his famous budget of 1909-1910, which provided a system of social insurance partly financed by land and income taxes, and he backed Asquith against the House of Lords when the upper House rebelled against the budget. The Lords had long been a favorite target for his darts. He called them "one-sided, hereditary, unpurged, unrepresentative, irresponsible, absentee," which, coming from a descendant of dukes, shocked the English aristocracy. The man was not only a dangerous radical, he was a traitor to his class. The attitude was not dissimilar to that of American Republicans in later years when they contemplated Franklin Roosevelt.

By what seemed deliberate sabotage Winston was jeered every time

Lloyd George, Chancellor of the Exchequer, and his friend on budget day.

he tried to speak in the House until he was obliged to complain to the Speaker of "conspiracy." All this was preparing the ground for future calamity. Hated by the most truculent sections of the working class, hated by the Tories, he was, said a contemporary, "the most hated man in politics," without a single section of the population on which he could rely for sustained support in an emergency.

No emergency arose, however, to put his position to the test and Winston drove ahead, backed by Asquith and Lloyd George. Marriage gentled him somewhat and softened his tongue, but he was rarely out of the news for long. As Home Secretary he set a precedent which has been followed by such excellent public officials as Mayor La Guardia of New York in being on the spot whenever any acts of God or man commanded the attention of the civil authorities. Winston was splashing in his bath when word reached him that a couple of sinister middle-European anarchists had holed themselves up in a slum in Sidney Street in the East End of London and shot down several bobbies. Winston called the military and rushed to the scene to direct the siege himself, hearing with enjoyment the familiar old sound of flying bullets. He was recorded in the act complete with fur coat and top hat by photographers cranking primitive movie cameras. For some reason nobody was amused. The new King George V was angry. Balfour asked in the House, "I understand what the photographer was doing, but why the Home Secretary?" The Home Secretary's innocent reply was exactly what might have been expected. "It was such fun," Winston said to an associate.

Irrepressible. He and Lloyd George stood out as the terrible twins of the political scene. They were two men with backgrounds as different as could be imagined. English aristocrat and obscure Welsh lawyer had joined in a historic friendship which survived many crises, but not all.

Winston and Lloyd George always spoke of each other with a high esteem laced with only the faintest flavor of *double-entendre*. Lloyd George is quoted as saying, "Sometimes when I see Winston

Winston directing the "Sidney Street Siege."

making these speeches I get a flash of jealousy, and I have to say to myself, 'Don't be a fool. What's the use of getting jealous of Winston?'" Of Lloyd George as Prime Minister in World War 1 Churchill wrote: "He possessed . . . a power of living in the present without taking short views. Every day for him was filled with hope and the impulse of a fresh beginning. He surveyed opinions, past utterances, or previous disappointments and defeats . . . This inexhaustible mental agility . . . was a rare advantage. His intuition fitted the crisis better than the logical reasoning of more rigid minds."

Herbert Asquith, the Prime Minister, had the task of keeping them both under leash in his Cabinet. From the dizzy heights of his birth and scholarship he wrote indulgently, "Our two rhetoricians, Lloyd George and Winston . . . have good brains of different types. But they can only think talking; just as some people can only think writing. Only the salt of the earth can think inside . . ."

(Max Beerbohm cartoon, 1911.)

The Tatler

Churchill: "Let's toss to see which of us will become Prime Minister if Asquith resigns."
Lloyd George: "But Winnie, would either of us as loser abide by the result?"

So dazzled were the couple by their own virtuosity that they scarcely noticed the appearance in the House in 1908 of a man representing the untroubled Tory seat of Bewdley, who came from a middle-class family made rich from industry. Nor was there any reason why they should, for he spoke only five times in his first six years in the House and had planned with his wife to give politics ten years and quit. Like Churchill he was an old Harrovian and there the resemblance ended. His name was Stanley Baldwin, and he was to confound both of them, Churchill and Lloyd George, and many others besides.

Winston's intellect and dynamism were such that mediocrity flinched and fled before him. Around him he was content only with the company of a small, quarrelsome clique of bloody-minded brilliants like himself. He formed a dining club with Lloyd George and with the lawyer and self-styled "verbal gladiator" F. E. Smith. A conservative M.P., Smith was one of the handsomest men in England and knew it, and he had an unerring talent for putting his contemporaries in their place with inverted epigrams. Of one of his friends he declared, "He always played the game and he always lost it." Of Winston he said, "He spent the best years of his life preparing impromptu speeches."

In 1911 Winston was given a further promotion and made First Lord of the Admiralty. By this time he was thirty-seven years old and running about three years behind his father in his sensational rise a quarter of a century earlier. Bemused by this second flash through the English political heavens, Sir Edward Grey, the Foreign Secretary, exclaimed, "Winston very soon will become incapable, from sheer activity of mind, of being anything in a Cabinet but Prime Minister." And a contemporary, John Morley, forecast that "if there is a war Winston will beat Lloyd George hollow."

He was a unique fellow all right, in many ways: in his appearance, his personality and the impact he made on the people around him. In a country and an era when first-naming was rare, he was invariably addressed as "Winston" and almost never as "Churchill," though this, as we have seen, did not betoken affection. In 1911 the public image of Winston Churchill was fully etched and it has changed little since. The smile had begun to peep out. It blossomed fully only when he became rubicund, but it budded faintly against the frozen wastes of his earlier gravity. He stooped forward, held his cane at the same slightly aggressive angle. His taste in clothes had been commented on in pained terms by the *Tailor & Cutter* magazine, although it really defied criticism. It was not so much slapdash as bred of a kind of dandyism *manqué*. He really cared. "Aha!" he cried to a journalist once. "You are the villain who wrote the other day that I was the worst-dressed man in London. . . . What awful rot you journalists write sometimes." He really cared, and if the effect was not quite what was originally intended, it was certainly inimitable. Or let us say rather that no one else ever tried to imitate it.

Two new weapons had begun to emerge when Winston went to the Admiralty. One was the torpedo-carrying submarine and the other the airplane. Churchill's enthusiasm for both, and especially the latter, was enormous. His colleagues were taken aback when he declared he intended to learn to fly himself. Winston said, with unusual lameness, that it would stimulate the profession of flying if the First Lord also learned to fly. The fact was that he just could not resist it. He began to take lessons in 1913. He flew in good weather and bad. Once he and his fellow pilot landed in a gale, and after alighting the plane took off by itself, blown by the wind, and crashed. The engines of the time were fragile and at the mercy of fortune. Winston at best, according to his flying tutors, was all right maneuvering in the air, but frightened his co-pilots rigid at take-offs and landings. He frightened the ground observers too. Only Winston, deep in concentration, cigar rammed into his teeth, seemed unmoved. Winston helped to form the Royal Naval Air Service, and thanks largely to his work England was the first country to

a Winston Churchill   Mat 1912

Winston Churchill in 1912, by Max Beerbohm.

The "flying fool."

mount machine guns in airplanes and launch torpedoes from them. Incidentally he credits himself with inventing the word "seaplane," and "flight" as a collective noun, meaning a given number of aircraft in organized formation.

The critics jeered and asked, in effect, what had all this stuff— airplanes, machine guns, etc.—to do with the Royal Navy, which lived by its super-dreadnoughts? Winston did not care. He never let any such inhibiting factor as the limits of his departmental responsibilities bother him. Fellow cabinet ministers would frequently read, with ambiguous feelings, long dissertations from Winston on matters that concerned them directly and him not at all. To the War Office he dispatched a memorandum giving his ideas of what form a future land war would take in the first days and weeks. His purpose was to make an intelligent estimate so that the heads of the fighting services could make their dispositions. It was a remarkable document based on the assumption that the war would involve Germany on one side and France and Russia on the other. He forecast almost to a day the duration and scope of the inevitable German offensive against France, how far it would penetrate into France, and when the French Army would be able to hit back. He also guessed what part the Russians would play in drawing off the Germans. General Sir Henry Wilson, director of military operations, dismissed the whole thing as "silly."

Winston's preoccupation with airplanes led directly to his interest in the possibilities of an armored vehicle which could cross trenches and move freely over pitted and torn battlefields. He felt such vehicles should protect his planes when they were land-based on the continent, and with naval funds he purchased some vehicles which were experimenting along these lines. Churchill never claimed to "invent" the tank, but by this action and his continued interest he made himself one of the pioneers in its development.

War had been in the minds of responsible ministers for a long time. Kaiser Wilhelm and his people, whose high virtues of industry, honesty and courage were discounted by their chronic servility, had shown their itch for trouble through a series of incidents and crises: the Kaiser's telegram of support to President Kruger before the Boer War, the German naval rebuilding program, the Agadir crisis in 1911 when Wilhelm decided to interfere in French activity in Morocco. It happened when no one expected it. On June 28, 1914, the Archduke Ferdinand of Austria, widely regarded as a warmonger, was murdered at Sarajevo in Serbia under circumstances that have never been fully explained, and the tensions increased as one by one the nations of Europe stepped into line in response to calls of treaty, lust or fear. The democracies vacillated as usual, but Winston did not hesitate. The Royal Navy, mobilized for its annual exercises at Spithead, he ordered to stay mobilized and be ready to move into action at an instant's notice.

One night at the height of the crisis Winston was at the Admiralty with some of his favorite companions. F. E. Smith, Max Aitken (later Lord Beaverbrook), the self-made Canadian millionaire, and a few others had gathered for an evening of cards. There had been a noisy but futile discussion of the international situation, and the men settled down to bridge. In the middle of the game a dispatch box was brought in for the First Lord's attention. Winston opened it with a skeleton key and from within he took a slip of paper which said simply, "Germany has declared war against Russia." From this moment step pounded on hammer step, each step more deafening until, with a roar of artillery, and a stamp of boots, the Great War began on August 4.

"Design for an Admiralty Christmas Card," by Bernard Partridge, satirizes Winston's expensive modernization schemes for the Royal Navy.

Part III

The World Crisis

The Sphere and Graphic.

First Lord of the Admiralty.

3

The World Crisis

IN 1914, AT THIRTY-NINE, WINSTON CHURCHILL WAS ALMOST SU-preme among British statesmen, First Lord of the Admiralty at a moment when, yet again, Britannia needed to rule the waves or perish. From the start he realized that he must maintain the most friendly and co-operative relations with the military. A new war, he foresaw, would be too enormous for petty interdepartmental rivalries. And how sincerely he worked at it! The example could well be read by service chiefs in Washington today. Being Winston, he set about the business of fraternization, on a strictly personal level. When the war began, he made his peace with Kitchener, who was soon regarding the "impudent subaltern" with approval. He was on friendly terms with Sir John French, the British commander in France, and even established a cordial relationship with the inveterate gossip General Sir Henry Wilson, director of military operations, who felt obliged to add in his diary when describing this accord, "I never liked him very much."

The Royal Navy was in splendid shape. Winston called back from retirement an imaginative old sea dog, Admiral "Jackie" Fisher, as First Sea Lord, and their partnership transformed and inspired the service. Both men were tireless, or to be more precise, tired at different times, Winston working through the night and Fisher through the day, Churchill writing his messages in red and Fisher in green, "just," said Fisher in admiration, "like port and starboard." The Navy moved the British Army to France without the loss of a single man. There they ran into the machine guns of the advanc-

Winston in the Admiralty office with First Sea Lord Fisher.

ing Germans and were slaughtered, for the Germans were sweeping on the Marne and threatening Paris, just as Churchill's "silly" memorandum had forecast.

The military situation was grim, and became grimmer as the Germans bulged outward toward Antwerp where King Albert and his Belgian Army were entrenched. The prospect of the Hun occupying a port facing England was not to be thought of. Kitchener summoned Winston to an emergency midnight conference of the defense staffs and it was agreed that a British statesman of stature be dispatched immediately to Antwerp with a force of Marines to reassure the Belgian King. Winston, ever pleased to volunteer for anything that smacked of excitement, set off, brushing up his quite unjustifiably confident French ("Intrepid Winston" said Asquith ironically). Eight thousand Marines landed and under Churchill's orders dug in. In a state of elation, Winston, cherubic in his Trinity House uniform, gesticulating violently with his cigar, calmed the fears of panicky Belgian politicians, ordered the brass hats here and there with a subaltern's relish. Back to London he sent a stream of reports and memoranda, and even offered to resign and take over the entire Antwerp forces, including the French and Belgian, in person "provided I am given necessary military rank and authority, and full powers of a commander. . . ." He had it all worked out, even down to his successor at the Admiralty. As Asquith commented in turning the request down, "Winston is an ex-lieutenant of Hussars and would, if his proposal had been accepted, have been in command of two distinguished major generals, not to mention brigadiers, colonels, etc. . . ."

Churchill returned to London. The Germans pushed and Antwerp collapsed. A thousand British casualties were reported, and 1500 more suffered the indignity of withdrawing into neutral Holland where they were interned for the rest of the war. It was a humiliating defeat, and the hopes built up in England by Winston's energy were cruelly dashed. Churchill was attacked bitterly in the press for what seemed a useless waste of lives. Not until long afterward did the experts realize and acknowledge that the Antwerp expedition had given the main forces of Britain and France time to get into position at Ypres and on the Yser. Antwerp was the first of the names that were to be spat into Winston's face for many years afterward by his enemies.

The Gallipoli campaign in 1915 was Churchill's way of winning the war at a stroke, and the tragedy still stings today when one thinks how nearly it came to succeed. By storming the Turkish-held Straits of the Dardanelles in one mighty amphibious action he hoped to open up a route through to the Black Sea to the aid of the gasping Russians, break the bloody deadlock which had settled on the Western Front since the Battle of the Marne, knock Turkey out of the war almost before she had entered it, hearten the Serbs, stay the Bulgarians from joining the war on the German side, and encourage the Italians and the Greeks to enter it on the Allied.

The operation began in February, 1915, with a fleet of 178 British and French ships which turned their guns on the outer Turkish

Gallipoli, from a Diorama by Denny C. Stokes.

forts of the Dardanelles in the greatest bombardment in naval history. Reports and intelligence were good and the British admiral forecast he would storm the Straits and batter Constantinople in fourteen days. He might have done it even more quickly. The allies did not realize to what depths of demoralization their bombardment had reduced the Turks. But in March the British and French navies moving in to probe the defenses ran into a minefield which blew up five of their ships. There was chaos among the admirals, who promptly decided that this should be an Army show after all. "Damn the Dardanelles!" Fisher exclaimed to Winston. "They will be our grave." Winston did not take him seriously. He had too much faith in the old sea dog. The generals could not make up their minds. The French were apprehensive that a military operation would weaken them on the Western Front, but Kitchener,

after weeks of disastrous dithering, agreed to release the necessary British and Anzac (Australian and New Zealand) troops, under General Sir Ian Hamilton. All the time the Gallipoli Peninsula, which runs like a finger down the northwest side of the Straits, was filling up with Turkish soldiers. A whole month was lost, and when the British and Anzacs went ashore they ran into the guns of a new Turkish army commanded by the German Liman von Sanders and a fine, new Turkish general, Mustapha Kemal. The soldiers gained a foothold and held it despite withering fire. There followed heartbreaking months of astounding losses and no progress. Had it not been for the delay the British must surely have won, and the face of the whole war would have changed.

In May, 1915, when prospects still looked good, Italy entered the war on the Allied side. By October prospects looked dreadful, and

Bulgaria came in on the side of Germany. The soldiers in the Dardanelles did not blame Churchill. The commander himself, Sir Ian Hamilton, confided his feelings to his diary and tried to contemplate what the campaign would be like if Winston were removed. "It would be an awful blow to us out here," he said, "it would be a sign that Providence had some grudge against the Dardanelles. Private feelings do not count in war, but alas, how grievous this setback to one who has it in him to revive the part of Pitt, had he but Pitt's place."

The Gallipoli Peninsula was not London. At home all the bats of fury flapped and squeaked around Winston Churchill's head. When it was seen that he was in trouble all his enemies came running. The French generals on the Western Front, backed by Sir Henry Wilson, were openly derisive, "The only way to win the war is to bleed the Boche," they said, "and the only place to do it is here in France." The fact that the French and British soldier was bleeding more profusely in the trenches than the German and that Kitchener was being forced to appeal to the nation for more and more recruits, remained obstinately irrelevant to them.

All Churchill's fighting instincts were aroused, but his position was a nightmarish one. He could not take command himself. Only the generals and admirals could do that. He stood at the pinnacle, encouraging, warning, advising, like a constitutional monarch, but unable to give directions on the spot. The Gallipoli campaign went on, a profitless slaughter on both sides, yet by its almost impersonal ferocity, uplifting—to Englishman, Aussie, New Zealander and Turk alike. Winston's confidence in the project was sustained. If only the soldiers could break through! Time after time the break was almost made, and then bad generalship or bad luck or both enabled the Turks to recover and counter-attack. And then, to Winston's horror, the man on whom he most relied turned to jelly. Fisher had behaved oddly from the start, blowing hot and cold by turns. At one point in the campaign he offered to go out and command

LORD KITCHENER
CALLS FOR MORE MEN

WAR OFFICE
WHITEHALL
S.W.

I have said that I would let the country know when more men were wanted for the war. The time has come and I now call for 300000 recruits to form new armies —

Those who are engaged on the production of war material of any kind should not leave their work. It is to men who are not performing this duty that I appeal —

Kitchener

NEW CONDITIONS OF ENLISTMENT.—Age Limit now 40.

Age- 19 to 40.
Height Minimum, 5 feet 2 inches.
Chest Minimum, 33½ inches.
Enlistment for General Service for the Duration of the War.

𝔊𝔬𝔡 𝔖𝔞𝔳𝔢 𝔱𝔥𝔢 𝔎𝔦𝔫𝔤.

the Fleet himself. Another time he tried to sneak out of a meeting of the War Council to resign but was hauled back by Kitchener, who reminded him that he was in a minority of one.

Winston found Fisher sliding away from him. He delivered an appeal to his old friend which resounds down the years in the immensity of its pain. "In order to bring you back to the Admiralty I took my political life in my hands," Winston wrote. "You promised to stand by me and see me through. If you go now at this bad moment and thereby loose upon me the spite and malice of those who are your enemies even more than they are mine it will be a melancholy ending."

Not only did Fisher desert Churchill, he sent an unsigned note, presenting his objections to the campaign, to Winston's most formidable enemy in the Commons, Bonar Law, an austere man of vegetarian leanings, who had been born in Canada and had followed Balfour as leader of the Conservative Party. At the same time Fisher resigned abruptly and fled to Scotland "to avoid further questionings."

In times of danger the British have an instinctive urge to end party politics, to form a coalition and present the enemy with a common front. The Conservatives were knocking hard on the door now, wanting in. In the face of the crisis they could even make harsh demands. And the first demand was that Churchill must go. Asquith was a civilized man. Over the years he had enjoyed watching his pet tigers, Lloyd George and Winston, at play. But the crisis was looming too darkly.

Perhaps because he was so deeply immersed in the day-by-day development of the crisis, Winston was taken by surprise when his resignation was suggested. Max Aitken, his close friend, who despite their many political differences had never failed to regard Winston with admiration in his moments of triumph, and with compassion in misfortune, said later, "Churchill was depressed beyond the limits of description." Lloyd George, equally, was appalled

As a result of Gallipoli he is forced to resign from the Admiralty.

by Winston's downfall and called it, later, "a cruel and unjust degradation."

Asquith kept Winston in the Cabinet for the sake of loyalty and continuity, but only as Chancellor of the Duchy of Lancaster, a post which technically exists to administer certain areas of Crown property but actually leaves the Minister free to do nothing at all. Balfour went to the Admiralty, and Lloyd George to the Ministry of Munitions where a first-rate scandal was raging over the shortage of shells for the Army. Lloyd George's star was still rising while Winston's had been abruptly extinguished.

Because history has so conclusively cleared Winston Churchill for his part in the sickening disaster of British arms at Gallipoli it is often forgotten how deeply into disfavor it flung him. The public cried out against him, and responsibility for the loss of British lives was laid at his door.

To Lord Riddell he confessed, "I am finished."

Clemmie Churchill moved the family from their apartments in the Admiralty to a flat at 41 Cromwell Road, Kensington, and Winston walked for the last time through the deserted offices at the Admiralty which he had graced with such promise of glory. All at once to the war correspondent Ashmead-Bartlett he cried out, the cry of a lion wounded but unbroken, "They never fought it out to a finish! They never gave my schemes a fair trial!" Those words uttered down silent and echoing corridors speak more perhaps for the spirit of the man than anything else he has ever said.

It is at moments like this that a man is most receptive to the generous gesture. Winston went to the Admiralty for the last time to put his papers in order, and, looking in awkwardly to say good-by, came Lord Kitchener. Still the idol of the masses, the Field Marshal was finding this war rather too much for him, and among sophisticates he was something of a joke. Soon the war would claim him too among the millions of dead. He was not good at small talk, but he chatted with Winston awhile, about this and that, then shook his hand and said good-by. "Well, there is one thing at any rate they cannot take from you," he said, "the Fleet was ready."

Winston had to make a choice. His seat in Parliament was constitutionally his until the next election. Did he, having entered the war as the chief of England's senior fighting service, wish to stay in the Government as a junior? The answer was No, and fortunately he had an alternative. He was a professional soldier with an international reputation for courage and enterprise. If there was no future for him in the Government—and he was certain that there was not—better go to France and take a command at the front. But first the long autumn of 1915 stretched out ahead while the political situation in London was untangled. He sat on the Dardanelles Committee examining the campaign which continued to drag on interminably.

For the first time in nearly ten years Winston was without a department to drive and time hung heavily on his hands. He had rented a house for the summer in Surrey. One day he saw a friend sketching, and the sight intrigued him. He bought some canvases and began to paint, at first tentatively and then with increasing confidence. Mrs. Churchill, happy to see him distracted from his troubles, encouraged him. Soon he was attacking his canvases in a rage of enthusiasm. Landscapes in blues, reds and oranges sprang under his brush and his spirits soared.

He returned to London to resign from the Cabinet. His farewell address was a long one, reviewing his record as First Lord of the Admiralty and ending, "I do not expect to address the Honorable Members for some time." The House sat on its hands. His reception was frigid, except for some cheers from scattered friends.

But, his decision having been taken, and with the prospect of excitement ahead, he felt in excellent condition. On the eve of his departure for France he dined with Lord Northcliffe, the newspaper magnate, owner of the *Times* and the *Daily Mail*, who found him "in great form and tearing spirits." He handed his diaries and docu-

© *Punch,*

CHURCHILL S'EN VA-T-EN GUERRE. (Winston [*through force of nautical habit, to Sir John French*], "Come aboard, Sir!")

"Plug Street" painted by Winston Churchill in 1916.

ments for posterity to the care of F. E. Smith, who was now Attorney General, then climbed into his uniform which he topped for no particular reason other than his own mysterious sartorial inclination, with a sky-blue French helmet.

In November, 1915, Major Churchill of the Oxfordshire Yeomanry, arrived in France and was welcomed warmly by his friend, Sir John French, who promised him command of a brigade once he had had experience of trench warfare. He was then promoted to Colonel and given command of the Sixth Royal Scots Fusiliers in the sector called Ploegsteert, corrupted by the troops to Plugstreet. But he was quickly reminded that he was a dog with a bad name. "You know," said a superior officer nastily, "we were not consulted on the matter of your coming to join us."

For his soldiers an eventful six months began. No sooner had Winston taken command than he sent out veteran scouts, experienced in the noble military art of scrounging. Back they came with delicacies to eat and warming fluids to drink, paid for either out of mess funds or, when those ran out, from Winston's personal account. Lobster and canned fruits graced the mess tables. Craftsmen carved and battered an old tin tub into a Venus's shell for him to take his bath, which he did with bursts of tuneless song, accompanied by records on an old gramophone which the batman cranked. In his spare time he painted war scenes and conscientiously studied aspects of war which he had hitherto neglected. Winston enjoyed trench life but several things about it nagged him. His stretch of the line was completely inactive except for occasional shellings. Winston was certain that German Intelligence must have learned the whereabouts of the former First Lord and he could not understand why they did not advance to extirpate him.

All Winston's old, hard-living Westminster cronies headed for his sector when they came to France on official junkets. Once F. E. Smith, the Attorney General, turned up and was arrested for having inadequate credentials. Winston watched his friend led shouting away. Winston wrote a chilly note to Bonar Law protesting such treatment to a person of F. E.'s eminence.

But even in his Plugstreet trench he was not immune from his enemies in Parliament. The Tories were still frightened about what he might do next. They remembered that he had hardly walked out of the Conservative Party and into the Liberal minority when an election reversed the position and he had become a Liberal Minister. He had recovered from a bad speech as Under-Secretary of the Colonies to leap the steps of promotion to the Board of Trade, the Home Office and the Admiralty. No politician in living memory had shown such a capacity to bounce back. He would not do so again if the Conservatives could help it. Bonar Law insisted to Asquith that Winston, in France, should play no part in the direction of the war. Otherwise, presumably, he would appoint himself Commander in Chief before anyone knew what he was about. Sir John French had promised him a brigade, but before 1915 was out

Major Churchill in 1916, painted by Sir John Lavery. Lady Lavery was one
of the first to encourage Winston to paint.

French was no longer Commander in Chief. Sir Douglas Haig, who had distinguished himself at the battles of Neuve Chapelle, Festubert and Loos, had taken his place and refused to honor his predecessor's promise, so Winston was left with his little battalion.

And at the other end of the scarred face of Europe, far beyond the trenches of France, past the Alpine war between the Italians and Austrians, past the campaign in Serbia, on the peninsula of Gallipoli, the last act of that great tragedy was being played. In December 1915 and January 1916 the Allies began to pull out. More than a quarter of a million British, Anzac, and French soldiers were dead, missing, or wounded out of 490,000 men landed. The Turkish losses were almost identical. The evacuation itself, a murderously difficult operation, was carried out almost without a casualty and was hailed as a victory. For such crumbs were the Allies grateful in those years of almost unrelieved gloom.

Winston was still a Member of Parliament and in March, 1916, he obtained leave to return to London to take part in a debate on the Royal Navy. While Lord Fisher listened impassively in the visitors' gallery, Colonel Churchill rose to plead for a new building program and for the recall of Fisher as First Sea Lord. Few then knew the inside story. One wonders what the seventy-five-year-old sailor must have thought as he listened to these expressions of magnanimity and patriotism from the young man of forty-one whose career he had done so much, through his weakness, to wreck. Churchill sat down. A Member called Meux who had made millions out of beer rose in reply, attacked the suggestion of recalling Fisher, and concluded, "We all wish him (Churchill) success in France and hope he will stay there." (laughter)

But that was just what Winston was planning not to do. Herbert Asquith, for all his intelligence and abilities, failed to inspire the confidence the people needed to sustain them in the face of constant military defeat. It was David Lloyd George whose speeches and performance thrilled the country. Changes were on the way,

Bonar Law attacking Winston at a meeting of the National Unionist Council.

and with them would come new opportunities perhaps for Churchill.

Winston's friends were urging him to return to the political scene, and his standing as an ex-minister made this a fairly simple matter. He was granted the necessary leave and his farewell address to the troops, if quoted correctly, was a remarkable one. "Whatever else they may say of me as a soldier," he proudly declared to his assembled men, "at least nobody can say I have ever failed to display a meet and proper appreciation of the virtues of alcohol." He returned to London in August, 1916.

In December Asquith was kicked out and Lloyd George became Prime Minister. It had been a feeble Coalition Government before. He was resolved to make it a strong one now. It is to Lloyd George's eternal credit that, facing a situation of crisis abroad and extreme delicacy in the House, he was determined to have his friend back. He could guess the fury it would create and he was not wrong. When he revealed his intentions the zombies screeched. The National Unionist (Conservative) Council, headed by Bonar Law, called an emergency meeting and resolved, by three hundred votes to two, that Winston's inclusion in the Government would be an "insult to the Navy and the Army." The "responsible" press was equally hostile. Churchill's inclusion, said the Sunday *Times* "would constitute a grave danger to the Administration and to the Empire as a whole." *The Morning Post* called him "Meddlesome Matty," said, "that dangerous and uncertain quality, Mr. Winston Church-ill—a floating kidney in the body politic—is back again in West-minster." Looking on, Max Aitken, also slated for inclusion in Lloyd George's Government, declared that never before in history had the selection of a Minister given rise to such opposition.

Was ever a man so hated? Bonar Law continued his vendetta against him unrelentingly. Lloyd George tried to beguile Bonar Law. If Winston is so dangerous, Lloyd George said to Bonar Law in effect, would it not be better to have him with you than against you? Bonar Law was not to be beguiled. "I'd rather have him against me every time," he said flatly.

What was Lloyd George to do? Winston had definitely been given to understand he would join the Government, but Lloyd George felt he would have to delay the appointment until the storm died away. On the night of December 5, 1916, Winston was dining with F. E. Smith when Max Aitken, according to his own account in *Politicians and the War,* turned up having just left Lloyd George. It was Aitken's painful duty to tell an exuberant Winston that he was not being included in the Government just at present, and for once that forthright man could not bring himself to speak directly. "The new Government will be very well disposed towards you," he said at last. "All your friends will be there. You will have a great field of common action with them."

Winston rose. "Smith," he said sternly, pointing to Aitken, "this man knows. I am *not* to be included in the new Government." And he walked out.

Lloyd George was loyal, however, and six months later he ap-pointed Winston to the important Ministry of Munitions, where-

Some members of Lloyd George's coalition government in levee dress: Winston Churchill, Lord Birkenhead, Lloyd George, Austen Chamberlain.

upon Winston faded into the background for the duration. It was Lloyd George, Lloyd George, Lloyd George all the way. Lloyd George unbending in the face of the bloodbath of Passchendaele and the U-Boat offensive, calm when the fiasco of Caporetto threatened to knock Italy out of the war, courageous over the collapse of Russia and the controversy over Jutland, and finally the Ludendorff offensive which almost won the war for Germany in March 1918. Students at the time had a favorite song of which the only words were, "Lloyd George knew my father! Father knew Lloyd George," sung to the tune of "Onward Christian Soldiers" and repeated ad infinitum with as many changes of tone and tempo as amused them.

Not that Winston was not busy at the Ministry of Munitions. After 1916 the French Army, which had borne the brunt of the fighting for more than two years, began to fade and more and more weight fell on the British and the Canadians. Munitions had to be rushed to France to sustain the bloody and usually abortive British offensives of 1917. Winston was, as ever, full of ideas, eager for action, tireless for movement. Flying was still his passion. He was certain that the air force was the key to the future conduct of military operations.

At the Aeronautical Research Laboratory at Farnborough he met an enterprising young scientist called Frederick Lindemann who possessed a rare ability to explain complicated scientific matters in simple English and under his guidance Winston became exceptionally well-informed on scientific affairs.

Winston would rise early to get his work done, then fly to France for conferences and return to his desk in London for the evening. These were still early days in flying and involved many hazards. Once, bound for London 2,000 feet up and over the Channel, a valve broke and the engine began to fail. It lost height and a crash into the sea seemed inevitable. When hope was almost lost the engine coughed briefly into life, long enough to get back to France. Winston climbed out and ordered another plane. Again they set off and again the engine failed over the Channel. This time they managed to glide in over the white cliffs of Dover and make a forced landing in a field. On another flying occasion the motors jammed and he crashed from a hundred feet. He was unhurt and addressed the House of Commons two hours later. On still another occasion his plane turned over and he and his pilot were suspended upside down.

The Russian revolution of February, 1917, coincided with a sudden crisis in relations between the United States and Germany. Neutrality, the policy which President Woodrow Wilson had set for America, had been growing more and more difficult to pursue. America had almost declared war in 1915 when the liner, *Lusitania*, was sunk with the loss of 114 American lives. The break now came, in February 1917, when Germany announced a policy of unrestricted submarine warfare, hoping to starve England out of the war before America could make her opposition felt. Two months later Wilson declared war, a decision that was rapturously greeted in England and France. "Bring on the American millions!" Winston cried in a speech, somewhat optimistically, because the American military contribution was negligible at first, and when the American troops began to arrive it was Winston's ministry which had to provide most of the munitions for them.

In 1917 the tank, which Winston had encouraged from the start, went into action for the first time and demoralized the Germans. Had the Allies possessed generals with the tactical sense to exploit it and the vision to see its value the war might have ended in that year.

When the great German offensive of March 1918 failed the end became a matter of time and from August 8 ("The Black Day of the German Army," said Ludendorff) onward the British with their tanks, the Canadian and Australian shock troops, the exhausted French and the newly-arrived doughboys of America rolled the so-far invincible Germans back before them. In November Germany capitulated and Winston on Armistice night was cheered by crowds of riotously celebrating Londoners as he made his way through the capital. From General Pershing he received the American D.S.C. for his work in supplying munitions to the Americans, or as Winston preferred to put it to his friends, "for distinguished service and gallantry in the face of the enemy, the latter qualification being waived in my case." He was the only Englishman to receive this award.

Winston's part as "the father of the tank" was given due acknowledgment, though he declined the financial awards which British governments hand out after major wars, on the ground—a laughable one so far as Winston Churchill was concerned—that he did nothing outside his own departmental responsibilities.

Winston with the Royal Family, Field Marshal Lord

Photo from European.

other senior officers at a victory parade in London.

The need for munitions was over. Lloyd George offered him the choice of either the War Office or the Admiralty, with the responsibility in either case for the Air Department. Winston chose the Admiralty so Lloyd George gave him the War Office anyway, with the tough task of demobilizing a huge army of tired and impatient soldiers as fairly and quickly as possible. There had been near-mutinies as the War Office had introduced a scheme to demobilize key technicians first. Winston quickly put a stop to that and changed the system to a more equitable "first-in-first-out" basis.

But a more gigantic problem faced Winston as War Minister. At the other side of Europe, the huge, sprawling, year-old Bolshevik Russian Republic had made peace with the Germans. In order to keep a fighting front going in the East the Allies had rushed soldiers into Russia to bolster the White Russian elements who rejected Bolshevism and were still loyal to the alliance. More than 60,000 Czech and Slovak soldiers had deserted the Austro-Hungarian Empire and had gone over to the Russians. These wanted to keep fighting the Germans. By mid-1918 there were British, American, French, Italian and Japanese troops in Vladivostok working cordially with Siberian soldiers, those purest and most engaging of Russians, who were serving under the White Russian Admiral Koltchak. Other allied troops had landed at Murmansk and were working with White Russian forces there. Four British Army brigades stationed in the Middle East had marched into the Caucasus to prevent oil supplies from going to the Germans. The question now was whether, since the Germans were beaten, should they be withdrawn?

The Big Four of the victorious powers, Wilson, Lloyd George, Clemenceau and Orlando of Italy, had gathered at Versailles to draw up a peace treaty, and were squabbling among themselves, Wilson refusing to recognize secret treaties reached by the Allies during the war, Clemenceau insisting on grinding Germany into the dust,

Reprinted by arrangement with David Low.

WINSTON'S BAG. He hunts lions and brings home decayed cats.

The Big Four at Versailles

Orlando demanding the territorial gains by which Italy had been bribed to enter the war in the first place. Russia to these statesmen seemed a long way away and when Winston asked for directions the replies he received were confusing. Yes, said Lloyd George, pull the troops out and leave the Russians alone to make their own destiny. No, said Clemenceau, crush the revolutionaries and keep in mind the huge French financial investments in Tsarist Russia. Winston agreed with the Frenchman. He detested the "foul baboonery of Bolshevism." Lloyd George sneered that Winston's "ducal blood revolted against the wholesale elimination of the Grand Dukes in Russia."

The White Russian armies went into action with some success, and Allied soldiers while doing no fighting themselves, co-operated.

Once it seemed that Moscow might fall to General Denikin's Whites, and Lloyd George only barely restrained Winston from hastening to the scene in person. "Winston wants to ride on a white charger through Moscow" he told a friend irritably, for he was angry at Winston's stand. Frustrated to be so far from the scene of action Winston spent his weekends blowing off steam by playing polo, an odd sport for a busy minister now forty-four years old.

All the time fighting went on, now favoring the Whites, now the Reds. But in face of public demand at home, British troops were withdrawn and so were the troops of the other Allies. Koltchak's armies disintegrated; Koltchak surrendered and was butchered in his cell. On January 3, 1920, Denikin's armies were decimated, and the fighting ended, leaving the Union of Socialist Soviet Republics with the Russian continent to itself, alone to take its uncertain but giant steps toward world supremacy. The Russians do not forget or forgive quickly. They would not forgive Churchill for what he had attempted to do.

Churchill's Russian intervention had lost few lives but a huge amount of money, and his relations with Lloyd George had cooled. Winston, after more or less winding up the responsibilities of the Ministry, hoped to be made Chancellor of the Exchequer. To his intense disappointment he was given the Colonial Office. Five months later, in June, 1921, his mother, Lady Randolph, died at the age of 67. To Winston she left the ceremonial robe of the Chancellor of the Exchequer which his father had worn when he occupied that position in 1886, and which she had treasured ever since. Churchill must have regarded this garment with mixed feelings.

As Colonial Minister Winston had to deal with a boiling Middle East, where, the Ottoman Empire having broken up, the Arabs, Zionists and British interests were setting up a cacophony of appeal and demand. Trouble and warfare had a habit of clinging to Winston's fingers like flypaper. In the summer of 1922 relations

A New Hat.

Courtesy of the Daily Express, L[...]

between Greece and Turkey exploded and the world paled at another crisis which threatened to burst into a major war. The Greeks probing into Anatolia were pushed out by Mustapha Kemal, who ordered his Turks to attack. The Greeks were routed, fleeing so fast the Turks could not catch up with them. Instead the Turks hurled themselves on the undefended Greek city of Smyrna to indulge in an orgy of looting and rape. They then wheeled, a hundred thousand of them, and bore down on Chanak, a strip of the Dardanelles thinly held by an Allied occupation force of English, French and Italian troops. The Turks piled up on the demarcation line, yelling and itching to overwhelm the small force which, under a courageous general, Sir Charles (Tim) Harrington, dug in and presented its line of bayonets.

To the horror of the Government in London, the French and the Italian governments ordered their own soldiers to withdraw, and the contingents, shamefaced, departed, hauling down their flags, watched in screaming glee by the Turks and glumly by the British. Only the Union Jack still flew. Winston was determined that the Allies should not be defied by a resurgent Turkey. He proposed to the Cabinet that military reinforcements and the Royal Navy should be dispatched to Chanak forthwith. His proposal was made public and once again it seemed that an incorrigible militarist was up to his tricks again. The combination of the two names, Churchill and the Dardanelles, was too much for public opinion to stomach. Meanwhile desperate diplomacy was at work, and in the middle of the crisis Mustapha Kemal backed down. The Turks withdrew.

The echoes of Chanak had hardly died away when there was a political crisis of the first order at home. The Conservatives, who since the war had been growing increasingly restive under Lloyd George's coalition, mutinied and voted in October to withdraw. Lloyd George promptly called a general election. But his own party was split in two between those loyal to him and those still loyal to

Mr. and Mrs. Churchill in Dundee at the General Election of 1922.

Asquith. The election caught Winston in the middle of an appendicitis operation and Mrs. Churchill campaigned for him in his constituency at Dundee, which he had represented as a Liberal since 1908. The vote, excluding a handful of grab-bag Independents and cranks, was as follows: Conservatives 344, Asquith Liberals 61, Lloyd George Liberals 53, Labor Party 142. Bonar Law's Tories were in with a clear majority, their first election win since the "Khaki election" of 1901. The Liberals were decimated, and in their place had risen a new and mighty force, the Labor Party, under Ramsay MacDonald, pledged to a policy of Socialism.

Overnight the face of British politics was changed forever. And the most startling single result of all was recorded in Dundee, which had Winston Churchill fourth in a field of five candidates, twelve thousand votes behind a Prohibitionist with the absorbing name of Edwin Scrymgeour.

Part IV

The Long Wilderness

LOST IN DUNDEE.

4

The Long Wilderness

"IN THE TWINKLING OF AN EYE," SAID WINSTON CHURCHILL, "I found myself without an office, without a seat, without a Party and without an appendix." He had controlled, in his time, the Navy, the Army and the Air Force. He had administered the Colonies, run the Board of Trade and the Home Office. He was known to be courageous in combat, morally fearless, colorful and brilliant. And an intelligent electorate had decided it preferred to be represented by one Edwin Scrymgeour.

What had happened? To be on the losing side was one thing. To be rejected so decisively in favor of a harmless teetotaler revealed a deep-seated distrust. Although seven years had passed, the mention of his name at any time during the campaign still drew cries of "Remember the Dardanelles," but that did not decide the election. It could only be that the voters had caught up with the sense of menace, of calamity even which Winston seemed to evoke, and which had already worried the most able and affectionate of his contemporaries. Time and time again it is reflected in the comments made on Winston by both his friends and his enemies.

"It is a pity," Lord Asquith said in his memoirs, "that Winston has not a better sense of proportion. I am really fond of him, but I regard his future with many misgivings. I do not think he will ever get to the top in English politics."

"Winston is often right," said Stanley Baldwin in a private conversation, "but when he is wrong—my God!"

"I think," said Bonar Law, in a letter to a friend, "he has very unusual intellectual ability, but at the same time he seems to have an entirely unbalanced mind which is a real danger. . . ."

Later on Baldwin said, "When Winston was born lots of fairies swooped down on his cradle with gifts—imagination, eloquence, industry, ability—and then came a fairy who said, 'No one person has a right to so many gifts,' picked him up, and gave him such a shake and twist that with all these gifts he was denied judgment and wisdom."

And Harold Laski, writing to Oliver Wendell Holmes, commented, "Unquestionably he has a real genius but he lacks staying power, and the egoism of his utterance would be appalling if he were not so obviously just a grown-up child."

On and on through Churchill's life the same theme runs: brilliant *but*, gifted *but*, eloquent *but*, possessed of genius—*but*. Even as far back as 1901 when Winston was only twenty-seven he both impressed and vaguely disturbed Cecil Rhodes. "He is a young man who will go far," said Rhodes, "if he doesn't overbalance." Everything he did created anxiety. Hidden motives were sought everywhere. Only Winston himself was unaware of it. He was shocked by the reverse. Returning to London from Dundee he stopped his car for a moment in Parliament Square and looked at the great mass of the Houses of Parliament. "Fancy," he said to a companion, "after a quarter of a century as an M.P. I have no right as a Member to enter the House."

It is a strange thing that ambition, which can be ungraceful and even ugly in a politician, was always engaging in Winston Churchill, which is surely due to his disconcerting but also endearing habit of identifying himself with England. In office he was happy as a sandpiper through the sheer enjoyment of handling England's affairs, although his colleagues tended to be less so, particularly when they received lengthy memoranda on matters which did not concern Winston's department at all. Others too were aware of his sense of identification. Lord Beaverbrook put it in a sentence in

Men in Power when, describing Winston's earlier eclipse in 1916, he said, "There were days when (Churchill) feared all might be lost if his services were denied to his country."

Bonar Law struggled along in poor health for six months before resigning, and he died shortly afterward. His successor at Downing Street was none other than Stanley Baldwin, the unconsidered tortoise of only a few years before. Had Winston stayed with the Conservatives in 1904 instead of switching to the Liberals he himself would have been leader of the Party and the Prime Minister. He had been happier as a Liberal than he had ever been as a Tory, but the thought of the conduct of England's affairs in the hands of Baldwin when they might have been in his own was undoubtedly a sobering one.

By this time, however, Winston had evolved a philosophy of eclipse and filled his time in a rush of painting, writing and constructive diversion. Until now he could say with just pride that he had not received a penny from anything except his own endeavors since he was a young subaltern. Now his great-grandmother, the Marchioness of Londonderry, bequeathed him a legacy of £40,000 and a handsome country house, Chartwell at Westerham in Kent. Here Winston painted for hours on end, and delighted himself in new forms of recreation and surrounded himself with dogs, swans, goldfish. He became fascinated with the art of bricklaying, applied for and received a bricklayer's union card.

Gathering around him a phalanx of secretaries, aides, and researchers, he threw himself into the production of his huge work, *The World Crisis*, which began to appear volume by volume. It was a sensational best-seller which was critically acclaimed for its weight of words, revelations and imagery, although Balfour described it gently as "Winston's brilliant autobiography disguised as a history of the universe." His financial situation suddenly and gratifyingly eased. Royalties on a hitherto unknown scale poured into his bank account.

Depite Winston's setbacks the record of his life was already a

Chartwell.

fabulous one. His literary stature in the English-speaking world was gigantic. Each new volume of *The World Crisis* as it appeared was greeted as ecstatically as the previous volumes. "It is full of grit and guts," said Harold Laski, who was no friend of Winston's. "One feels he has never had half an hour's quiet reflection in his life, but he has certainly lived every moment of it."

Winston concluded the story of the war with the words, "Surely, Germans, for history it is enough." No impersonal reflection this, it was a personal exhortation coming from Winston Leonard Spencer Churchill wagging the finger of his country. In other words, learn the lesson of the war. Consciously or not it mirrored the maxim of Bismarck that "the politician has not to revenge what has happened but to ensure that it does not happen again."

But for all his activities Winston viewed the political picture with growing alarm. Some of the scenes which followed the 1922 elec-

118

tion, though comic, were ominous, particularly the antics of a group of newly elected Scotsmen from the Glasgow area, the "Red" Clydesiders. A comrade with the appropriate name of Newbold, elected as a Communist, cabled Lenin, "Glasgow won for Communism." In Glasgow station the crowds cheered a new Westminster-bound Socialist who shouted, "When we come back this station and this railway will belong to the people." (His name was David Kirkwood. It has to be added that Davie died a peer and a Privy Councillor.)

Winston himself was a sincere radical, who had been damned only fourteen years before as "a traitor to his class," but his radical feelings were largely paternalistic and combined with an innocent sense of compassion. "Fancy living in one of those streets," he said to a friend while campaigning once in the Manchester slums, "never seeing anything beautiful, never eating anything savory, never saying anything clever."

Socialism with its steely apparatus of the massive union, the free use of the strike weapon, the instinctive sympathy with Soviet Russia, was not to his taste. To his dismay he saw that Asquith's Liberals were beginning to nuzzle uncomfortably close to the Labor Party. Should they come together, what, he asked himself, would become of him. Then Baldwin, at the end of 1923, forced an election on the issue of Free Trade or Protection. Lloyd George and Asquith moved temporarily together to fight him, and Winston, his Free Trade blood up, campaigned with the Liberals. There was no point in fighting Dundee again. The Liberals gave him West Leicester where he fought an earnest feminist and suffragist, Frederick Pethick-Lawrence. He lost again. The result of the election was that the Tories won 225 seats, the Liberals 159, and the Labor Party 191.

No side had a clear majority, and Asquith decided to throw his support to Ramsay MacDonald and enable him to form the first Labor Government. Here was a new and exciting figure to emerge as Prime Minister. A pacifist during the war, he was idolized inside the Labor Party. They called him "Ramsay Mac," a name which

"Ramsay Mac."

by its special avuncular sound signaled the warmth of their affection. MacDonald combined a glorious Scots voice with the beauty of a silent movie star. Blond hair tumbled over a craggy Celtic face luxuriantly mustached. Here was another man who had outpaced Winston Churchill to the pinnacle of political life.

Winston missed the clang and battle of politics. Beaten by a clown like Scrymgeour, beaten by Pethick-Lawrence who had run out of intellectual puff when he helped women to get the vote, Winston had to prove that he was not, at the age of forty-nine, a political has-been. He had no alternative now but to quit the Liberals, whom he had served faithfully for nearly twenty years, and return to the Tories—if they would have him. A special election came up in a gilt-edged Tory division of Westminster. The Conservative Central Office appointed a Tory to run for it against three other strictly second-division candidates. Winston decided to stand too, as an independent, an obviously hopeless task. He called himself a "Constitutionalist," and gathered about him the most unlikely band of supporters to help him. In his own words, "Dukes, jockeys, prize fighters, courtiers, actors and businessmen all developed a keen partisanship. The chorus girls of Daly's Theatre sat up all night addressing envelopes and dispatching the election address. It was most cheerful and refreshing. . . ."

First reports had Winston in. At the Foreign Office young Duff Cooper, a rising figure in the political-social world, married to one of England's great beauties, Diana Manners, read the tapes and sent off a telegram of congratulations to Winston, after which he departed to celebrate with a good lunch. Returning to find that Winston had been beaten by forty-three in a poll of 23,000, Duff Cooper wrote apologizing for the error and added that he hoped to serve under him when Winston became leader of the Conservative Party. This letter is remarkable for one thing. It is perhaps the only expression of confidence in Winston's future penned in that period.

The election, however, showed that Winston was still a political force and he was officially welcomed back by the Conservatives. Almost immediately the Liberals and the Socialists broke their alliance on the question of a loan to the Soviet Union and the nation went to the polls again for the third time in two years. This time Baldwin's Tories won by a landslide and the Liberals were obliterated forever from the British political scene. The election gave the Tories 412 seats, the Socialists 151, and the once-mighty Liberals just 40. Lloyd George held his seat but was cast away into the wilderness never to return. Asquith retired to the obscurity of the House of Lords, as Earl of Oxford and Asquith, while his witty wife, Margot, with a mildly scandalous autobiography on the best-seller list, settled down to wield her pen even more fiercely. Winston, after three defeats, was back in Parliament again. His enemies watched his new comeback in baffled rage.

Stanley Baldwin, firmly in office for the first time with a massive majority and five comfortable years to go, sent for Winston. It was an ironic confrontation—the West Country squire, smooth as a priest from easy victories and untroubled progress, face to face with the scarred veteran of a quarter of a century of political triumphs and disasters, now a rebel redeemed. Baldwin, amused within himself at the bombshell he had prepared, asked Winston if he would serve under him "as Chancellor."

Winston expected no more. "Of the Duchy of Lancaster?" he asked, thinking of the Cabinet post without duties which he had briefly held under Asquith when he was kicked out of the Admiralty.

"No, of the Exchequer," said Baldwin. Tears came to Winston's eyes. Why did Baldwin give to Winston the most important job in the land after his own, why also did he give the Foreign Office to Austen Chamberlain (Joe Chamberlain's son), and the India Office to F. E. Smith, who had become Lord Birkenhead in 1922, two other men whose power drive was in such contrast to his own instinctive lethargy? These were appointments both magnanimous and astute. Baldwin's critics hold that he felt himself safer with these

Lord and Lady Asquith.

thunderbolts on his side rather than against him, that he particularly feared, in view of his own comparative lack of experience, an alliance against him of Lloyd George and Winston Churchill. A simpler solution is also available, and does more credit to Stanley Baldwin. Queried by Harold Laski, Baldwin said simply, "Winston is the ablest mind in politics."

The appointment spread despair through the ranks of Labor, who considered Winston their arch-enemy, and fury among many unforgiving Tories. Would the man simply not stay down when he was out? Back in 1917, barely a year after the fiasco of Gallipoli, he was restored to favor as Minister of Munitions. Yesterday he was without party or even seat. Today he was Chancellor of the Exchequer.

Winston donned his father's robe, regretting only that his mother had not lived to see him wear it. One of his first acts in his new job was to put England back on the gold standard for the first time since before the war so that, in the expression of the times, "the pound could look the dollar in the face." This had been the aim of the Treasury and the Bank of England ever since the war and Churchill should not be blamed exclusively for it, but it was a bold and, as it turned out, a disastrous move. Churchill's numerous critics of the time included the economist J. M. Keynes, who wrote a pamphlet called *The Economic Consequences of Mr. Churchill.* Churchill was warned that the pegging of the English currency at the prewar value of gold would price British exports out of the international market.

His critics declared that he combined a too-rigid nineteenth-century idea of the value of English money with an inadequate knowledge of arithmetic. Lord Randolph, as Chancellor, had complained of "those damned dots" and Winston did not seem to give the impression of being much more confident. This was not his finest hour.

England's most important export was coal, and business in the

Courtesy of the Daily Mail, London.

THE TOPPER. Now, That's Something Like a Hat.

mining areas declined. For a while the Government managed to keep the miners' wages up by subsidies to the coal owners, but subsidies could not be extended indefinitely and when it seemed that the miners might be abandoned by the Government the other unions rushed to give them moral support. The atmosphere became heavy with suspicion. Baldwin and his ministers began negotiations with the miners, both sides knowing that a breakdown could result in only one thing—a general strike and the gravest domestic upset in centuries, almost certainly accompanied by violence and bloodshed with Briton pitted against Briton. Only a spark was needed. Winston Churchill supplied it. Word reached him at 11 o'clock on the night of Sunday, May 2, 1926, that some of the printers at the *Daily Mail* office had gone on strike rather than print an editorial critical of the unions. It was not this fact but the headline—"For King and Country"—which bothered the printer who saw no reason why either King George V or Great Britain should be invoked on the side of the employers.

The Cabinet was in session. He took the news to Baldwin, who was furious. What seems in retrospect a trivial incident was magnified by fear and physical weariness into a declaration of war. The Government demanded that the unions repudiate this act. The unions declined and on May 4 the General Strike began.

Five million British workers downed tools. Cheering, inspiring them, was a new figure in British affairs, whose flat staccato voice united the whole British working class movement with its matter-of-fact power and common sense. His name was Ernest Bevin. "Even if every penny (of union money) goes," he declared thumping his fist into his hand, "and every asset is swallowed up, history will write that it was a magnificent generation that was prepared to do this rather than see the miners driven down like slaves." This brought his hearers yelling to their feet and at the same time Bevin could make his halls ring with jeers by the mention of one word, "Churchill!" Churchill had started it all. Churchill had "seen red"

Ernest Bevin.

over the *Daily Mail* dispute and deliberately made Baldwin intractable. Down with Churchill!

This was war and Winston was in the middle of it, both fists flailing. He ordered out the military in case of trouble, but his appreciation of the English character was at fault, for there was no trouble. Pickets were generally orderly, and, in fact, the strikers, inspired by their own unity, were in excellent humor. In Plymouth strikers and policemen played a soccer game, the strikers winning by three goals to one.

Almost all news had stopped. The newspaper plants were empty and picketed. Except for a trickle of copies of the *London Times* and the strikers' sheet, the *British Worker,* no papers were to be had. This gave Stanley Baldwin an idea. He was worried about Winston's furious energy and felt it ought to be channeled constructively. One night Diana Cooper, the beautiful wife of Duff Cooper, telephoned Clemmie Churchill to find out what were the latest developments. What Clemmie told her made her go pale. "Winston is *what?*" she exclaimed.

The Chancellor of the Exchequer had become a newspaper editor. Winston had moved to the offices of the *Morning Post* and was rattling off copies of a new journal, the *British Gazette.* Troops and police patrolled the plant on the lookout for sabotage. Visiting firemen kept turning up at all hours of the day and night just as they had done at the Plugstreet trenches in France. Workers and visitors were given special passes and no one was allowed to enter without one. Winston was always elaborately scrupulous in presenting his pass to the guards at the gates. Then one evening Lord Birkenhead, the Secretary of State for India, appeared, handsome as a god in full evening dress, and swaying ever so slightly after an admirable dinner. He searched his pockets perfunctorily and could not find his pass.

"Sorry, sir," said the guard, "but I can't admit you."

"Don't you know who I am?" said Birkenhead with hostility.

Lord Birkenhead.

"I do, but I have my orders."

"Do you think I am going to undress at this time of the night to find the damn thing? Tell Churchill I am here."

This was too much for Winston. He remembered the time his old friend had been conducted firmly from the trenches. F.E. had clearly to be saved from himself. Winston rushed to the entrance, had him admitted, then, ignoring F.E.'s indignation, clamped two guards on him with instructions not to allow him out of their sight.

Not for a long time had Winston enjoyed himself so much. He stood among the presses—his presses—and listened to the sweet music of their roar, walked among the compositors and linotype operators bent over their tasks. He noticed a pitcher of beer by the side of each man.

"Have they got enough?" Winston asked.

"Yes, sir," said the overseer.

"Nonsense," said Winston, handing over a pound note, "send for more."

In a week the circulation of the *British Gazette* jumped from 200,000 to more than two million and began running out of paper. Impatient to pile on a larger and still larger readership, Winston appropriated the paper supply of the *London Times,* to the indignation of Geoffrey Dawson, that newspaper's illustrious editor, who complained to the Prime Minister. Stanley Baldwin was reading Winston's daily outpouring in growing consternation. On every page and in every issue Winston was slamming the trades unions, his heavy guns drowning out the stodgy arguments of the *British Worker.* To the strikers the image of Churchill was rising to fiend-like proportions. "For heaven's sake," Baldwin said to Geoffrey Dawson, "give Winston some tips on how to produce a newspaper. Make it out in a letter to me." Dawson did so. Winston replied with a letter of his own on the principles of newspaper production which Dawson had to confess in some delight was "great."

On May 12 the strike ended in complete victory for the Government, and the left-wing *New Statesman* ungagged itself with a burst of fury against the *Gazette*. "It was supposed to be supporting the authority of Parliament," the magazine raged, "but gave us nothing worth calling a report of the proceedings either of the House of Commons or the House of Lords. For that we had to go to the *Times*. . . . It was scandalous that the *Times* should have been deprived of its paper supplies in order to enable Churchill to poison public opinion. We can only offer our congratulations to the *Times* for the struggle which it made in the face of this robbery. . . ."

Winston was not unaware of the shortcomings of his newspaper. In the House he turned a face of thunder to the Socialists and pointed at them. "I warn you," he shouted over the snarls opposite, "if there is another General Strike"—the rumbles of resentment grew louder—"we will let loose on you another *British Gazette*." The anger melted into laughter on both sides of the House, but the resentment of the working classes did not soften.

Ernest Bevin certainly was in no mood to forget the strike with a laugh. "It is not that Mr. Churchill is not a brilliant man," he said bitterly, "but it is not safe to leave the destinies of millions of

131

Rage in the wilderness. Lloyd George seven years after he
ceased to be Prime Minister.

people in the hands of a man with an unstable mind, a man who can fly off at a tangent as he did in the war with such terrible results to millions." It was the familiar echo, that inevitable *but* again.

The nation recovered from the strike and the Government continued its fairly confident way. The atmosphere in the Cabinet was good and Baldwin was content to let his team have its head. Sometimes his indolence infuriated others, particularly Neville Chamberlain, son of Joe and half-brother of Austen, who was Minister of Health, a conscientious, indefatigable man who pecked away at his work as busily as a hen after grubs. Once Chamberlain was making a lengthy report to the Cabinet and noted in irritation that Baldwin seemed to be scarcely listening. The Prime Minister reached lazily for a sheet of paper, scribbled something, and passed it to Winston who chuckled. Chamberlain looked across. What it said was "MATCHES. lent at 10.30 A.M. Returned?" Chamberlain stopped in the middle of his report and protested violently.

This suggested not only an amicable relationship between Baldwin and Winston but also an attuned sense of humor. It did not last, it could not. Time is the enemy of all Cabinets, good and bad. Tensions and ambitions come to the surface as time goes by and teamwork frays as an election approaches. In 1929, with a new election coming up, the first in five years, Winston was still the second most powerful man in England. He knew it, and so did his colleagues, who resented it. His relations with Baldwin declined.

Baldwin, discussing the Tory prospects for the next election with Neville Chamberlain, was not optimistic. Baldwin foresaw a stalemate between the Conservatives and the Socialists with Lloyd George and his handful of Liberals holding the balance, in which case the King might ask Lloyd George to form a Government. "The King's Government must be carried on," said Baldwin, "but I personally will not serve under L.G."

Chamberlain said that neither would he.

"In that case," said Baldwin, "the leadership will go to Winston."

Both men looked at each other and grimaced. They talked of "Churchillian domination" and neither relished the prospect.

And, in fact, it did not materialize. The election of 1929 put another feeble Labor Government under Ramsay MacDonald into power, obliging Baldwin, Churchill and company to move to the opposite side of the House. By the British system Winston still enjoyed considerable standing. He remained in the "Shadow Cabinet" which the minority party maintains in anticipation of its eventual return. But relations between Baldwin and Churchill were worsening daily. Winston had had enough of Baldwin, who, as his confidence in himself as a parliamentarian increased, found less and less need for disturbing alliances with men too clever for his own good.

Every party has its own built-in vices which defy time and experience, death and birth, growth and decay, and the vice of the English Tories is a periodical and recurring yearning for mediocrity. Baldwin had fought the urge for five years and now he was succumbing, eyes closed, pipe puffing, to this dream of a nerveless, idea-starved state of non-thinking. It was not indecisiveness. On the contrary, Baldwin and his supporters were very decided. They were, in Churchill's words, "decided . . . to be undecided, resolved to be irresolute, adamant for drift, all-powerful for impotence."

Winston could not stand it. He resigned from the Shadow Cabinet. Political resignations are usually on some comparatively minor issue, the small rash reflecting a deep-seated disease. Officially Winston resigned over the India Bill which sought to guide India by gentle degrees to Dominion status. Winston was not an expert on India (who was?). The India he knew was the India of his subaltern days, a Kipling's India and *The Story of the Malakand Field Force*. He despised Gandhi, whom he called "a seditious Middle Temple lawyer posing as a fakir of a type well known in the East, striding half-naked up the steps of the Vice-Regal Palace . . . to parley on equal terms with the representative of the King-Emperor," but his record as Colonial Secretary and his support of an honorable peace for the Boers had already shown that he was not among the die-hard school in Imperial affairs. The resignation over a wise and honest bill was not characteristic of Winston Churchill, and it can only be explained by the fact that he had already had enough of Baldwin.

In 1931 Britain was caught in the full blast of the American crash. Ramsay MacDonald united with Stanley Baldwin to form a Coalition Government to "save the pound." In Ramsay MacDonald, described by Churchill bitterly as "the boneless wonder," Baldwin had an ideal comrade, a left-wing counterpart to Baldwin himself. MacDonald combined with his physical beauty the vanity of Rudolph Valentino. His Labor associates were horrified by the deal he had made with the Tories, but MacDonald did not care. His gorgeous voice uttered nothing but the most enervating platitudes. He talked about the country going "on and on and on and up and up and up." Like Baldwin he had a profound distrust of action of any kind, and the presence of Tories in his Cabinet gave him a heaven-sent excuse to put off yet again the Socialist reforms his party had set its heart on since its inception. He had been a pacifist in the war and he had sung the "Red Flag" in the General Strike. By 1931 he was giggling that every Duchess in the land wanted to kiss him. The union of vanity with lethargy was a dispiriting one, and as MacDonald and Baldwin surrounded themselves with an increasing assembly of second-raters there was no room for Winston Churchill.

Winston was now close to sixty and had served in every office in the Government except that of Foreign Secretary. He had had every chance and he had lost out to others. If there was no more place in the conduct of British affairs for Lloyd George why should there be for Winston Churchill? Baldwin was relieved to see Winston out of his conclaves, but he also watched his decline with sorrow. Baldwin liked Winston, and his comments, both in private and in public, were rarely ungenerous to him. He, like the rest of the people in British political life, was convinced that Winston's career was over, and that future generations would remember him as a writer rather than as a politician.

In this entire period the extraordinary prophecy of Duff Cooper that he would serve under Winston when he was the leader of the Tory Party shines like a beacon. And this makes all the more remarkable the forecast of another political figure who was watching British affairs from a far oriental distance.

In 1931, when Churchill's political fortunes were as low as they had ever been, Joseph Stalin found himself confronted by Lady Astor who was taking her first—and last—look at Moscow. The Lady from Virginia opened her audience with the words, "Mr. Stalin, do you read the Bible?"

Stalin had no intention of being diverted by trivialities. He changed the subject and asked about Churchill, what he was doing, and what were his prospects. "He is finished," said Lady Astor, not without relish. She told the Russian dictator he could forget about Churchill, write him off. "I do not agree," said Stalin. "You will send for the old war horse yet on the day of battle."

This would certainly have cheered Winston up had he known about it. He was not so philosophical. In fact he was in the blackest depths of despair. "I have cheerfully and gladly put out of my mind all ideas of public office," he said, and one can imagine with what a heavy heart he gave such tragic notice of abdication, he who loved the responsibilities of office with such passion. "I felt sorry for him," said Robert Vansittart, head of the Foreign Office, rather unfeelingly, "because he felt so sorry for himself."

As usual, a Churchill denied expression in government expressed himself in writing. In 1930 he wrote a charming memoir called *My Early Life*, ending with his marriage, "after which," he said, "I lived happily ever after." In the thirties he poured out an impressive flood of magazine and newspaper articles which placed him beyond competition as the highest paid free-lance writer living.

Charlie Chaplin with the Churchills at Chartwell, September, 1931; with them, the second Earl of Birkenhead (who had succeeded his father in 1930), Diana and Randolph Churchill.

At Chartwell, where he lived with his handsome family, he entertained many of the most famous figures in the world. He particularly enjoyed the company of Americans. Bernard Baruch, a close friend of many years' standing, was a regular visitor. Alfred Smith dined there after his Presidential defeat by Herbert Hoover. Over dinner at Chartwell Winston gave Charlie Chaplin a theme for a movie in which Chaplin would play Napoleon, returning to France incognito from St. Helena or Elba, the French believing him dead. Chaplin stewed over the idea for several years, but did nothing about it.

Winston set off for the United States on a lecture tour which was, however, rudely interrupted in New York City. On his way to Bernard Baruch's house he stepped off the sidewalk on Fifth Avenue and 67th Street, and instinctively looked right rather than left. The British determination to keep their traffic rolling on the

137

On the books: LIFE OF MARLBOROUGH

On the paper: National Defence

© Punch, Lon[don]

"It was a great Work, and I wish you could now add another chapter to your own career."

different side of the road from the rest of the world has probably done for more Englishmen abroad than any number of foreign wars. Winston was abruptly deposited into the gutter by a fast-moving taxi-cab and transported to Lenox Hill Hospital with a sprained shoulder and multiple lacerations. Finding himself with time on his hands he dictated an article about it and sold it for $2,500.

All the time he was being urged toward a task which was to have a vital influence on his outlook, and indeed, according to some, on his whole personality. Arthur Balfour and other friends were persuading him to attack the enormous volume of papers in the Blenheim archives, and write a definitive biography of the Duke of Marlborough. Churchill agreed. He assembled around him the usual relays of secretaries to take the stream of words as he dictated them, and researchers and archivists to check his manuscripts, and labored at his task through the night and into the small hours of the morning. His life of Marlborough proved to be a monumental work, running to four volumes, not so much an objective biography as a detailed vindication of a man much maligned in his lifetime and by biographers. Winston was frank about his intentions, which were "to examine every criticism or charge which the voluminous literature on this period contains, even when they rest on no more than slanderous or ignorant gossip."

The result was something more than a masterpiece. It was a notable exercise in self-revelation. As he wrote, much of his surface arrogance seemed to fade, the chips fell from his shoulder. One can sense that he was not thinking of Marlborough alone when he wrote:

> It is said that famous men are usually the product of unhappy childhood. The stern compression of circumstances, the twinges of adversity, the spur of slights and taunts in early years, are needed to evoke that ruthless fixity of purpose and tenacious mother-wit without which great actions are seldom accomplished.

It would be pointless to speculate whether Churchill's ideal image changed during the course of writing his book from that of his father to that of his most distinguished ancestor, except that the conclusion has been drawn by some of his most intimate contemporaries. Leo Amery, always an honest friend, said that in writing his life of Marlborough Winston "found his true model . . . the fusion of political and military ideals, as well as the inspiration of family piety, for which he had all his life been groping."

Meanwhile in Germany Brownshirts were gathering in torchlight processions; ruffians, freebooters and class riffraff, marching under the swastika flag to the orders of a rabble-rousing Austrian psychopath, Adolf Hitler. On January 30, 1933, he came to power. On February 27 the Reichstag went up in flames. Hitler used the excuse to suppress the Communist Party. Soon he began a rampage of persecution against the Jews, denounced the Treaty of Versailles imposed by the Allies in 1919, all in crude, guttural gutter talk which notwithstanding seemed to play all the chords of evil hitherto suppressed in the German personality. Never before in history had such a grotesque clown been allowed to come to power with so little protest from a so-called civilized people.

Churchill awoke to this violent new power in Europe with a start. He dreamed of "great wheels revolving and great hammers descending day and night in Germany." He warned the House in March, "I dread the day when the means of threatening the heart of the British Empire should pass into the hands of the present rulers of Germany." Baldwin merely smiled and puffed his pipe. The Germans had found their political ideal, and so had the British.

Make no mistake about it, Baldwin spoke for England, the England of the mid-thirties. Baldwin, with his John-Bull face and the pipe which he rubbed reflectively on his nose, with his comfortable wife, the cricket-watching, pig-patting countryman was the embodiment of a country which wanted to turn its back on Nazi Germany, hoping that if you didn't look at it it would go away. Shortly after Hitler rose to power Oxford undergraduates held a famous

Stanley Baldwin.

debate. The motion was: "In the next war this House will not fight for King and Country." The motion was carried. Young Randolph Churchill, Winston's son and an Oxonian, was deeply mortified by this demonstration of adolescent puerility. Since Oxford had not won the annual boat-race against Cambridge in years, his father simply wondered in apparent bewilderment what was the matter with these young men "who can't row and won't fight."

Baldwin is remembered mostly to history as the man who won the election of 1935 by deliberately deceiving the electorate over the state of Britain's defenses. Meanwhile Winston Churchill, now just an ordinary Tory M.P., who was warning of the appalling truth of Britain's nakedness as he had warned from the start, was shouted down in the Commons. England was not the only country to blunder into disaster on such hazy dreams of complacency and *laissez-rien-faire*.

141

Against this danger Churchill warned day after day. In 1935 he began his undying series of speeches urging rearmament. The Labor benches listened with reluctant respect, while from obscure corners at the back of the chamber, Tories clucked and howled, making funny noises whenever he rose to speak. Thirty years is not too long in political memory and there were influential figures who still resented Churchill's departure to the Liberals in 1904. British political organization is oddly dictatorial and authoritative. Winston was too eminent to be disciplined himself. Nobody dared touch him. But every young Tory M.P. who privately expressed himself in favor of Churchill was threatened and bullied by the powerful Party machine where he was weakest—in his own constituency. The local Tory committee, backed by the Conservative Central Office in London, reminded the Member in as many words that he was in the House on their approval alone, and that if he did not mend his ways there were many able, personable, aspiring politicians on the waiting list ready to take his place at the next election. This was "the gentlemen of England," as Professor A. J. P. Taylor puts it, "playing dirty as only they know how to do."

There was also the "Cliveden (pronounced Clivden) Set," the group that met at the country home of Lord and Lady Astor. Politicians and writers of all shades of opinion met at Cliveden, but one thing all the regular Cliveden weekenders agreed on was the appeasement of Germany. This was the policy on which the Set fed. It was a breeding ground of political gossip and speculation which sought to destroy the enemies of appeasement at home with epigrams.

The battles between Winston and Lady Astor were long and furious. There is a famous anecdote which has been told of the fiery Virginian-turned-Englishwoman and several other politicians. Consuelo Vanderbilt gives the man's role to Churchill. "If I were your wife," Lady Astor roared at him, "I would put poison in your coffee." To which Churchill replied with dignity, "And if I were your husband I would drink it."

Lady Astor with Geoffrey Dawson, leaders of the "Cliveden Set."

Altogether these were a dangerous and depressing set of enemies for a man trying to awaken England to its own mortal danger. As a group they were summarized by one of the politicians of the era, Lord Percy, who confessed in retrospect that "gusto was what we lacked; the best of us were a low-spirited lot; and our low spirits sapped our capacity for the best kind of political leadership."

Lloyd George had gone right over to the enemy. He had met Hitler and had been enraptured by him. "Fuhrer is the proper name for him," he said to a friend. "He is a great and wonderful leader . . . the savior of Germany," and in a newspaper article on his return to London he called him "a born leader of men, a magnetic dynamic personality with a single-minded purpose." He declared at the end of the article, "Everywhere (in Germany) I found a fierce, uncompromising hostility to Russia coupled with a genuine admiration for the British people, with a profound desire for a better understanding with them. The Germans have definitely made up their minds never to quarrel with us again."

L.G. had held no office since he was Prime Minister and his long absence had told tragically on his judgment and character. He had become vindictive and full of hate, imperiously unforgiving: "It is rather sad," wrote J. M. Keynes, "that after all these years he is quite unable to be philosophical and look back on the past with a little regret, a little wonder, a little large mindedness. . . ."

As the figure of his old chief declined, Winston's grew larger. It was Winston, not Lloyd George, who now appeared as the unique figure of British public life. Everyone who despaired over Baldwin's blindness turned to him, including some of the most important figures in the administration. Civil servants, diplomats, scientists, military men—all those who saw and could prove the preparations Germany was making for war—kept Winston informed, often in secret, knowing that he would make the maximum use of it in the House of Commons and in his newspaper articles. When Winston warned that German aircraft production was catching up with Britain's and would pass it in 1936 he was revealing what he knew to be true even if he could not reveal his source. Chartwell in Kent was as well informed as the Foreign Office in London, Winston the best-informed statesman in Britain, Baldwin included.

The standard of the Cabinet under Baldwin sagged lower and lower. When Hitler repudiated the Treaty of Locarno in 1936 and moved his troops into the demilitarized Rhineland, Baldwin gave in to public pressure and agreed to appoint a Minister to co-ordinate the country's defenses. Everyone expected him to choose Winston. He chose instead a minor politician, Sir Thomas Inskip. When the announcement was made one statesman insisted with assurance that it was a clerical error. Another declared that "There has been no

Photo from European.

Mrs. Simpson and the Prince of Wales in 1936.

similar appointment since the Roman Emperor Caligula made his horse a Consul," and it is said that one aged lobby correspondent fell off his chair in a dead faint.

In 1936 England took time off from Hitler for its two-week plunge into the Abdication crisis, and once again Winston Churchill was in the middle of it. The story of the Abdication has been told many times now. Edward VIII, the King of a few months, had been, as Prince of Wales, the most idolized figure on the face of the earth. He was determined to marry a middle-aged American woman who had been twice through the divorce courts. Baldwin had always distrusted the heir to the throne. In fact many of the senior politicians shook their heads over inside reports of the Prince's indiscretions, his choice of friends, his relations with the Royal Household. The Prince of Wales fell off horses the way Winston Churchill crashed airplanes. Both men meant one thing to the established order of English society, trouble. Their appearance or even the mention of

145

their names made old clubmen wince over their *Morning Posts* and hold their breath as though expecting the sound of heavy thuds and the shattering of glass.

Even as far back as 1927 Baldwin had accompanied the wilful Prince to Canada to seek some way of communicating common sense to him. He failed and the future of the monarchy haunted the Prime Minister until it became a nightmare. When the Abdication crisis exploded Baldwin found a miraculous opportunity to get Edward off the throne completely. The King's two chief supporters were Lord Beaverbrook and Winston Churchill. Beaverbrook, publisher of the London *Daily Express*, had been fighting a private war unsuccessfully against Baldwin for years and saw that by backing the King he might unseat his old adversary at last. Churchill, on the other hand, may have felt a somewhat kindred spirit in the Prince. Edward VIII was a *but* man too, and in his own way a rebel against mediocrity. He was colorful *but*, glamorous *but*, a great advertisement for the English monarchy and Empire *but*.

At first British public opinion was inclined to favor the King's romance, but Baldwin's handling of the crisis, apparently so patient, in reality so implacable, swung the nation round to his side. And he was obviously right. He was fighting for a standard of conduct and discipline that a King simply could not flout. When Winston rose in the Commons to plead that Baldwin take no irrevocable decision without consulting the House he was howled down with such venom that he sank to his seat staggered and abashed. The *Times* with some pleasure reported that it was the worst rebuff in modern political history.

Baldwin again spoke for England, although England did not know his motives, and he did not hesitate to deceive the country, the King, the House of Commons, even his Cabinet, but never himself. Publicly he played the role of a man giving his utmost to persuade the King to follow his duty and renounce his hopeless love affair. Privately he was determined that the King should go.

An early picture of Winston and the Prince of Wales.

The Abdication.

For one frightful moment Baldwin thought he had been over-persuasive. "Only time I was frightened," he confessed to a friend. "I thought he might change his mind. But I need not have been. He had given his word (to abdicate) and that was enough."

After the abdication, Churchill and Beaverbrook were talking over old times and Churchill, according to Tom Driberg in *Beaverbrook*, had said that though they had often been wrong, one of the two had always been right.

"That's easy," said Beaverbrook. "We always differed."

"Except once," Churchill reminded him.

Beaverbrook laughed. "Perhaps we were both wrong that time," he said.

On a note of personal triumph Baldwin witnessed the Coronation of King George VI, who was to prove a noble and a notable monarch, and then he retired, rich with glory. To friends Baldwin talked about his life, his friends and enemies, with the gentleness of an elder statesman confident of his place in history. He had been in power a long time and had defeated Winston and Lloyd George repeatedly in debate and in political maneuver. "Lloyd George and Winston," he said pityingly at the end, "the flotsam and jetsam of political life thrown on the beach."

Few men have retired to a chorus of more general acclaim and affection. "Now he has gone," effused Beverley Baxter, the journalist M.P., who was unfailingly loyal to every Tory Prime Minister in succession no matter how hostile they were to each other. "Now he has gone. The beloved dictator has departed, not in defeat, but at the height of his powers and the triumph of his career. He will be unchanged by loss of office as he was by its acquisition. But he will be happier. . . . The greatest Englishman of our time will ask nothing more than to live the remainder of his years as a citizen of the country which he loves so deeply and which he served so well."

Three years later Baldwin was to be sitting staring blankly into the fire, and contemplating that he had, in the words of his official biographer, "seen affection . . . and admiration converted into the bitterest hatred and to know that far and wide throughout his own England men and women under the rain of death were cursing him. . . ."

On Baldwin's advice the new King George VI called on Neville Chamberlain to form a government. Although their names are often linked together Chamberlain never spoke for England as Baldwin did. He and England happened to meet at one terrible moment in the crossroads of history and then they parted. Chamberlain was a proud, brave, self-centered, nasty old man who was never in Baldwin's class. Physically—and especially placed against the strutting dictators, Hitler and Mussolini, or even the tough little Provençal, Daladier, Prime Minister of France—Chamberlain was a dismaying sight, with his rolled umbrella and his small, scrawny cock's head sticking out of his wing collar. To make matters worse, when he smiled he seemed to smirk, which added to his air of disdain. Where Baldwin was lethargic, Chamberlain was the busiest of bees. He was convinced that a meeting with Adolf Hitler would solve everything. He had a high opinion of Winston Churchill—"unlike L.G., Winston never bears malice," he said—and he planned to find a place for Churchill in his Cabinet. But surveying the bland, smiling faces of the men around him at the Cabinet table, he decided how much more tranquil it was without Winston than with him. The old fear of "Churchillian domination" crossed his mind again, and Winston was left out.

Worse still, he began to plan to rid himself of the two remaining first-class brains in the Baldwin Cabinet, Anthony Eden at the Foreign Office and Duff Cooper at the War Office.

Eden was unpopular in Berlin, and in November, 1937, while Eden was away at a conference in Brussels, Chamberlain quietly arranged for Lord Halifax to go to Germany. Ostensibly Halifax

Neville Chamberlain with Anthony Eden.

Winston faces his "darkest hour."

Kemsley, from P

was going as a master of fox hounds to visit a hunting exhibition. *"But incidentally,"* as one of the Cliveden friends twittered to an acquaintance, "he will visit Hitler."

The visit was a political sensation in the West and everyone turned to Anthony Eden to see how he would take this snub to his authority. But of course Eden was not even in London, and the London correspondent of the *New York Times* cabled excitedly home that "the decision to send Halifax to Berlin represents a clean-cut defeat of the Foreign Office, and at the same time of Mr. Eden. . . . He and his advisers have been overruled, not for the first time, by a small but powerful group in the Cabinet. . . ." Two months later Eden resigned on a technicality, and Winston Churchill, seeing almost the last wise head go, was reduced to despair. "I must confess," he said, "that my heart sank and for a while the dark waters of despair overwhelmed me. In a long life I have had many ups and downs. . . . But on this night of February 20, 1938, and on this occasion only, sleep deserted me. . . ."

Beverley Baxter compared Eden's resignation to the Abdication crisis and commented, "Both Eden and King Edward had the benefit of Winston Churchill's close advice before taking the final decision, and in each case Churchill attacked the Government and showed his willingness to form an alternative administration. Winston Churchill remains the most brilliant failure of political history —a man who could not pick a winner with only one horse in the race."

A few days later Hitler occupied Austria and incorporated it into the German Reich. On that same day Joachim von Ribbentrop, then Hitler's ambassador in London (and a very popular one with the hostesses), was dining with the British Cabinet. Winston had been invited too, nobody knew why. Winston himself thought perhaps "they asked me to show him (Ribbentrop) that, if they couldn't bite themselves they kept a dog who could bark and might bite."

The occupation of Austria was followed by the Czechoslovakian

Chamberlain at Berchtesgaden.

crisis and the tragedy of Munich, in the middle of which Duff
Cooper resigned in disgust. Germany, having swallowed Austria,
began in the summer of 1938 to threaten Czechoslovakia. As long
ago as 1936 Lloyd George had said, "I wish Neville Chamberlain
could be closeted with (Hitler) for half an hour," thinking they
could solve everything. Chamberlain elected to do just that. He
talked to Hitler and he capitulated. He told the Czechs to yield
their frontiers and defenses to Germany or take the consequences.
Czechoslovakia, a courageous, martial, and democratic country, had
an alliance with France and Russia, but France dared not move
without England, and Russia glowered and said nothing. The Czechs
gave in.

Daladier had attended the Munich conference with Chamberlain. When he returned to Paris he saw a crowd gathered to greet
him, and turned his collar up expecting to be pelted with rotten
eggs for his betrayal. He found to his amazement that he was

Hitler bidding farewell to Chamberlain after the Munich conference. Between
them, Sir Nevile Henderson, British Ambassador to Berlin and
Dr. Paul Schmidt, German Foreign Office interpreter.

cheered. Daladier at least had the intelligence to understand within himself the shame of his act. Not so Chamberlain. He returned to London accepting the cheers of relief as his automatic due, declaring he had achieved "peace in our time."

In the House the Tories greeted him deliriously. Victor Raikes, M.P. for South-East Essex, declared that "there should be full appreciation of the fact that our leader will go down to history as the greatest European statesman of this or any other time." Doggedly Winston rose to his feet amid the howls and catcalls that had become the normal accompaniment of his remarks. Through a storm of protest he said, "I will begin by saying what everybody would like to ignore or forget but which must nevertheless be stated, namely, that we have sustained a total and unmitigated defeat, and that France has suffered even more than we have."

"Nonsense," cried Lady Astor. But this time Churchill was not alone. He was supported in the Commons not only by Eden and Duff Cooper, but by Clement Attlee, leader of the Labor Party, and Sir Archibald Sinclair, leader of the Liberals. Throughout the country there was a painful conflict of emotions. The English had been literally in a sick, physical fear of war, but even as they cheered they were ashamed they cheered, and soon the cheers died away altogether and only the shame was left. The nation's soul began to emerge. Winston's position in British affairs was shifting curiously. He was, for the first time, becoming really popular, nay, he was becoming the spokesman for more and more sections of the British public, including those who had esteemed him least. The British working classes had sized up Hitler a long time ago. The middle classes had supported Munich but they too revolted against their own fear. All turned to Churchill.

Only Chamberlain, still backed by the Cliveden Set and the Tory M.P.'s, went his unruffled, assured way. The Fuhrer had declared at Munich that his territorial aims were at last satisfied, and Cham-

Chamberlain, Mussolini, Halifax, Ciano.

berlain quoted this smugly. Asked how he could accept the word of a man who had broken it so many times, Chamberlain replied, "This time he promised me."

Now it was Mussolini's turn. The Italian dictator was Hitler's one major potential ally. In January, 1939, Chamberlain and Halifax visited Rome. Mussolini was pursuing his own dreams of a new Italian Empire in the Mediterranean, and, hoping to tire the elderly British statesman into easy concessions, laid down a gigantic program of sightseeing and dining. The celebrations went on day and night through a non-stop chorus of *"Viva"* from the crowds. When the visitors were not standing stiffly at attention through interminable national anthems they were shaking multitudes of hands. Endless rows of Blackshirts were drawn up with daggers bared on either side of endless ribbons of red carpet. But to Mussolini's surprise, deepening to dismay he saw that Chamberlain was tireless, flourishing even. Consequently the conference fell rather flat. Mussolini listened dejected to long Chamberlain harangues

157

"ANY TELEGRAM FOR ME?"

translated by a sulky Count Ciano. Halifax thought with pleasure that the Duce had "mellowed." He hadn't. He was just dead beat.

Six months after Munich in March, 1939, the Germans occupied Czechoslovakia. When the news arrived Chamberlain said he felt as if he had been cheated at cards, which was not much consolation to the Czechs. Too frightened to guarantee a strong and brave land, Britain was now galvanized into activity and was ready to guarantee everybody. Appeasement was finished, the Cliveden Set dead. Chamberlain was not. Seldom has a political leader faced the failure of his own policies so repeatedly as Chamberlain without acquiring even a touch of humility.

The cry for the return of Churchill to the Cabinet now came from almost every section of the country, with the exception of the House of Commons. There the Party discipline still prevailed and the Tory M.P.'s were warned not to associate too closely with Churchill. Instead the organized anti-Chamberlain group tended to cluster round Anthony Eden, who was considered less of a hell-raiser.

But a new England was arising now from the death of Czechoslovakia. Baldwin's England had died and Churchill's was being born. Chamberlain was aware neither of the death of the one nor of the birth of the other. Geoffrey Dawson of the *Times* wrote in his diary for July 6, 1939, "Went down to the House for a brief talk with the Prime Minister. He is full of vigor and has no intention of being bounced (sic) into taking back Winston."

Chamberlain's dilemma was genuine enough. The Germans hated Churchill with all their impressive capacity to hate. To appoint Winston to the Cabinet would be little short of a declaration of war. "The nearer we get to war the more his chances improve," he protested testily to a friend. "If there is any possibility of easing the tension and getting back to normal relations with the dictators I wouldn't risk it by what would certainly be regarded by them as a challenge."

The rape of Czechoslovakia had brought renewed demands for an anti-German alliance with Russia. The cry came particularly from France who recognized then, as indeed she does today, that she needs Russia to hold the Germans back, that the logical consequences of being anti-Russian can only be to have the Germans sooner or later overrun her country. But while Chamberlain sent a Foreign Office functionary to Moscow, Hitler sent his Foreign Minister, von Ribbentrop, who concluded the Hitler-Stalin nonaggression pact which doomed Poland, knocked the vinegar out of the French, and left the Western allies to engage in a war under hopeless disadvantages.

At 5.30 P.M. on September 1, 1939, the German tanks rolled across the Polish frontier, shot the legs off the Polish cavalry horses and stormed for Warsaw. It was what England had been waiting for. Now the call for Churchill must surely come. The trouble was that with Chamberlain you never could tell.

Courtesy of the Daily Express, London.

The Invasion of Poland.

Part V

Glory and Disillusion

Mr. Churchill returns to the Admiralty.

5

Glory and Disillusion

THE FORTY-EIGHT HOURS BETWEEN SEPTEMBER 1 AND SEPTEMBER 3, two days almost forgotten by history, confirmed the worst fears of the nation. On September 1, Chamberlain sent Hitler an ultimatum to withdraw. On the second he said he would not recognize a German annexation of the port of Danzig. But the declaration did not come. He was like a small boy giving a bigger boy until he counted ten to back down and then counting "eight, nine, nine-and-a-half, nine-and-three-quarters, nine-and-seven-eighths. . . ."

The war-hungry populace and the House of Commons were going crazy with frustration and anger. They cried even louder for Churchill but unfortunately his voice had been most effectively silenced. Chamberlain had finally asked him to join the war cabinet. Churchill accepted and as a result he could not publicly speak against the Government. But private memoranda flew. "Aren't we a very old team?" he wrote Chamberlain. "I make out that the six you mentioned to me yesterday aggregate 386 years or an average of 64, only one year short of the old-age pension."

There was no reaction at all from Downing Street. Winston stormed around his apartment in Morpeth Mansions, Westminster, in a fury. Chamberlain, busy with his own problems, ignored him.

Finally, on September 3, Neville Chamberlain did manage to get out a declaration of war. He bewailed Hitler's lack of faith and restated his own attempts to preserve peace. It was hardly warlike, but at least he had done it. France dragged even more slowly and did not declare war until half a day later. Two nations less fierce

The Sinking of the Graf Spee.   *Wide World*

could scarcely be imagined. The only indications the British people
had that they were at war was an air-raid alarm (a false one) on the
first day and that Churchill was First Lord of the Admiralty again.

On September 17 Russia entered the stricken Poland from the
east and carved the country up amicably with the Nazis. Even with
most of the Wehrmacht in Poland the French Army showed no disposition to get up and go on the offensive. They sat in the Maginot Line
with drooping morale, developing not only pasty faces but a most un-
wholesome fear of Germans. The British went into a casual mobili-
zation, with the slogan "Business as usual." Only Churchill seemed
to be making an effort, in the same office in which he had sat in
1914. Once again the Navy was ready. There was one bad defeat
when a U-Boat penetrated into Scapa Flow, Britain's great naval
fortress, and sank the *Royal Oak*. Otherwise the U-Boats were kept
under control, and German merchant shipping was swept from the
seas. Winston was all for sending the Royal Navy into the Baltic on
a great naval offensive, but was reluctantly dissuaded by his appalled admirals. When the Navy forced the *Graf Spee* to scuttle
herself after being bottled up by three smaller and out-gunned British ships in the harbor at Montevideo the nation welcomed her first

166

real victory and Winston danced a figure in delight in the Admiralty. Next British sailors led by Captain Vian armed with cutlass, boarded the German prison ship *Altmark* to liberate English prisoners.

But these were isolated efforts. There was no sparkle to the war effort. Duff Cooper noted in his diary, "Winston told me Chamberlain doesn't take him into his confidence. They meet only across the table. There is obviously no love lost between them."

Chamberlain himself, however, was thoroughly happy with the conduct of the war. He was already over seventy and suffering from gout, but still he adored his job, and he was eager to absorb more and more responsibility. His speeches were ill-prepared, sloppily worded and commonplace. In the spring of 1940 when he announced complacently that "Hitler has missed the bus," the assertion did not seem to be based on very much and shortly afterward became one of the unluckiest remarks any Prime Minister ever made.

The Germans struck, swallowed Denmark overnight, invaded Norway and compelled an Anglo-French expeditionary force to withdraw almost as soon as it had landed. Hitler had missed the bus, indeed! A furious House packed itself in like sardines to debate the conduct of the war. Even as they spoke Hitler's Panzer divisions were moving west by night toward the borders of Holland and Belgium. The Members did not know this but they knew they were in a real war at last and Chamberlain was leading England to defeat.

Winston's friends, feeling the explosive atmosphere of the House, were nervous. The Royal Navy was not without blame for allowing the Germans to invade Norway from the sea, and they feared that Churchill might go down with Chamberlain. Also they feared that should the House spare Churchill, his sense of justice would make him spring all the more furiously to the defense of his chief. Members electrified by the gravity of the occasion spoke as they had never spoken before. Duff Cooper pleaded with M.P.'s not to listen to a word Churchill would say. "He will be defending with his eloquence those who have so long refused to listen to his counsel, who treated his warnings with contempt and refused to take him into their confidence. Those who so often trembled before his sword will be only too glad to shrink behind his buckler."

Chamberlain, his acrid mouth downturned contemptuously at the corners, appealed to his friends in the House—"and I have friends in the House"—to stand by him, a deplorable choice of words in view of the catastrophe lunging toward Britain. Lloyd George replied savagely. The former Prime Minister had been long in the wilderness but tonight he was back at his best. "The Prime Minister has appealed for sacrifice," he said. "The nation is prepared for any sacrifice so long as it has leadership. I say solemnly that the Prime Minister should give our example of sacrifice, because there is nothing which can contribute more to victory in this war than that he should sacrifice the seals of office."

Churchill, as his friends had feared, replied bitterly. "He (the Prime Minister) had a good many friends when things were going well," pleaded for an end to dispute. "Let all feuds die. Let all the stray horses be pulling on the collar," and warned that a precipitate vote in a moment of difficulty was unworthy of the British character. Lloyd George was up again smiling. "The Right Honorable gentleman," he said, "must not allow himself to be converted into an air-raid shelter to keep the splinters from hitting his colleagues."

It fell to little Leo Amery to climax the debate. Over the years he had been a stalwart in the Commons and had held high office, without ever really touching or aspiring to greatness. He had opposed Churchill's budgets and Churchill's views on India, but like so many others he realized that the nation could be saved only by Winston. He repeated to Chamberlain the terrible adjuration of Oliver Cromwell. "You have sat here too long for any good you have been doing," he cried. "Depart, I say, and let us have done with you. In the name of God—go."

Chamberlain glared back at him, his teeth bared in his small mouth. He was full of fight and courage, and he refused to yield.

Lloyd George shows his old greatness again.

The scenes as the M.P.'s went to vote on the vote of confidence were fantastic. It was impossible to keep the Conservatives in line. Conservative after Conservative defected. Some were shedding tears. One sang "Rule Britannia." Chamberlain's majority when the vote was counted dwindled from the expected two hundred to eighty. Scores of Tories had abstained and many actually voted against their leader. It was a thundering demonstration of no confidence. Chamberlain walked out of the House a dumbfounded but far from broken man, and this being England and these Englishmen, the hate against him welled into sorrow and a grudging admiration.

Churchill loved debates like this whatever their outcome and could not have been in higher spirits. Members hollow-eyed after the late-night sitting saw him at six o'clock in the morning bubbling over, putting away a large plate of fried eggs and bacon and smoking a huge cigar. He looked, as one observer said, as if he had just returned from an early morning ride.

Two days after the debate, on May 10, 1940, Hitler struck in the West, invaded Holland and Belgium, who screamed to Britain and France for help, and Chamberlain, his voice almost lost in the din, agreed to resign.

Churchill's moment had almost arrived. Historically it was inevitable. Time and time again England, a sea power, had been drawn into military campaigns against great armies and always, out of her need she had been able to summon the one man whose qualities she knew would save her—the man too independent, raucous, stubborn, clever to be worth the trouble of coping with in peacetime. There had been Pitt the Elder against Napoleon, Palmerston in the Crimean War, Lloyd George in the first World War—and now Winston Churchill.

But first there was an astonishing moment of uncertainty. Chamberlain asked Churchill to see him in Downing Street, but he invited Lord Halifax too. Churchill listened as Chamberlain asked Lord Halifax if he thought he could form a Government. Halifax was deprecating. As a member of the House of Lords he was forbidden to enter the Commons, which meant he could be at best only an honorary Prime Minister. Halifax, as long and lean as the Ancient Mariner, was a solemn man but he possessed both goodness and a sense of humor. "Churchill," he commented afterward, "with suitable expressions of regard and humility said he could not but feel the force of my words. The Prime Minister reluctantly and Churchill with much less reluctance accepted my view."

So Chamberlain, in accordance with British constitutional practice, went to King George VI and advised him to send for Churchill, and Winston became Prime Minister even as Hitler was sweeping through Belgium and dropping his paratroopers on Rotterdam. Winston was sixty-six years five months and eleven days old. Other men had caught up with and passed him a long time ago. Mussolini had been in power since 1922, Stalin since 1924, Roosevelt since 1932 and Hitler since 1933. Baldwin had been Prime Minister at fifty-six and MacDonald at fifty-eight. Now Winston's day had arrived, and the great era of this turbulent life was about to begin.

And what an era; so brief and yet in its brevity it blinds history with the intensity of its light! For essentially it lasted for only one stupendous year. Beginning on May 10, it ended, in its grandest sense, on June 22, 1941, when Hitler invaded the Soviet Union. It was a year of exaltation on the part of the British people, of majestic speeches and assured control by the new Prime Minister, of a colossal effort in the factories and on the high seas, of courage and burstingly high morale in the homes.

Party politics were forgotten. The coalition Cabinet Churchill formed included two men who, with Churchill himself as Minister of Defense, were to give the conduct of the war its most driving impetus. The Socialist, Ernie Bevin, his old enemy, was made Minister of Labor, and the violent isolationist Tory, Lord Beaverbrook, his old friend, Minister of Aircraft Production. Lord Halifax stayed at the Foreign Office for the time being to keep a continuity in foreign policy, with Anthony Eden waiting in the wings for a respectable interlude. Leo Amery was given the India Office, Duff

Cooper the Ministry of Information. Frederick Lindemann came to his side as his personal assistant. Lloyd George was offered a post but declined. His great night in the Commons was done and the Welshman was played out. He retired to the country to his own dark defeatist thoughts and was not heard of again.

To the Commons Winston promised only "blood, toil, tears, and sweat." The military situation could not have been worse. It was catastrophic beyond the worst nightmares of generals and politicians. Holland was knocked cold in four days. Belgium stayed in the war for two weeks and surrendered. The Channel ports for which the British had sacrificed hundreds of thousands of lives in the first World War were occupied. By reaching the sea at Abbeville the Germans cut the Allies in two. Most of the British Expeditionary Force with some French detachments were bottled up in a steadily diminishing pocket inside Belgium, separated from the main French Army to the south. Only the port of Dunkirk, on the border of Belgium and France, was left and the trapped Allies fell back in an apparently forlorn hope that they might be rescued by the Navy before the Wehrmacht overwhelmed them. More than 350,000 men were caught in the trap. Against the terrific weight of German armor the British had almost no anti-tank guns left and even fewer tanks. Churchill's military advisers warned him that at most 20,000 to 30,000 men might be re-embarked. The rest were doomed.

But at Dunkirk a miracle was happening. In answer to Admiralty appeals Englishmen in trawlers, yachts, pleasure cruisers, and seaside "Skylarks" were sailing out under continuous dive-bombing attacks and bringing the British Expeditionary Force back, 338,000 of them, their equipment left behind, beaten but no longer green; hard battle-scarred veterans, the elite core of a new and better British Army. Among the generals who came out from Dunkirk for example were General Alan Brooke, General Alexander, General Montgomery, General Dempsey, General Anderson and others representing the nation's best military potential. The cheerful *London Daily*

Winston Churchill's Finest Hour.

"The Withdrawal from Dunkirk," by Charles Cundall.

Mirror expressed the whole thing in a headline of two words,
BLOODY MARVELOUS!

Hitler watched them go with a sneer. "They will not come back
again this war," he said. His high opinion of the British had evapo-
rated before the war started. "Our enemies are little worms," he said.
"I saw them at Munich." But he had not met Churchill at Munich.
Hitler for the moment was not interested. He was after richer prize
than the puny British Army. Pausing only a few days to regroup
he sent his tanks and dive-bombers ahead again and the Hun smashed
his great military fist into the face of an already weeping France.

Time after time Churchill flew to Paris to bolster the politicians,
but was met with abuse, appeals, hysteria, and hopelessness. He
could not believe it, that these people, in some cases the very same
men, men such as Petain and Weygand, who had fought so well
in the first World War, were so paralyzed by fright in the second.
He sent General Sir Bernard L. Spears to France to try to keep
the country in the field. Spears loved France almost as much as
he loved England and grieved to see soldiers he respected thinking and then talking in terms of surrender.

Then Paris fell, and Italy declared war on England and France.
It was too much. On the morning of June 18, 1940, when France
was on the point of asking for terms, Spears, exhausted and in despair, found himself waiting for an aircraft to bring him back to
England. He chatted awhile with a youngish French general whom
he had met several times and who was a friend of Prime Minister
Reynaud's. The soldier had distinguished himself even in this in-
glorious campaign by commanding the Fourth French Armored
Division with considerable local success against numerically superior
Germans. His name was Charles de Gaulle. To Spears he said, "I
have no intention of surrendering." Spears gulped and grabbed him,
pulling him inside the aircraft.

The following night the same officer, tall and somewhat uncertain of his position though not of his destiny, spoke to France over

the B.B.C. and said, *"Moi, General de Gaulle, soldat et chef francais, j'ai conscience de parler au nom de la France. . . ."*

England was alone now. A country unarmed waited while the Germans, from Narvik to the Pyrenees, and with a reluctance which Britons did not then know, prepared to cross the Channel. "We are fighting by ourselves alone," Churchill said on July 14, Bastille Day, "but we are not fighting for ourselves alone. Here in this strong City of Refuge which enshrines the title deeds of human progress and is of deep consequence to Christian civilization; here, girt about by the seas and oceans where the Navy reigns; shielded from above by the prowess and devotion of our airmen—we await undismayed the impending assault."

The British in their new mood of dedication and ferocity wanted to get rid of everybody associated with Munich. Neville Chamberlain, though a dying man, was still in the Cabinet, and attacks against him, against Halifax and others grew so vicious in the press that Winston became alarmed that it would hurt the country's morale. He called Cecil Harmsworth King, the newspaper publisher, to Downing Street and talked to him about it. Churchill explained his personal position. It was true that he was Prime Minister but one incident in the House of Commons had impressed him that his position was far from unassailable. When he and his new Cabinet met the House it was Chamberlain who had drawn the bigger cheer from the Tories. The Munich men were everywhere, Churchill said, not only in politics, but among the generals and admirals and the civil service chiefs. To clear them out would be impossible. If one turned only to those people who had been right in the previous years, what a tiny handful he would have to depend on! King's paper, the *Daily Mirror*, had been most violent in its attacks on the Munichists. Churchill told him flatly he was not going to run a government of revenge. If people did not like his Government they could form another one and God knows where they would get it from—he wouldn't serve on it.

Unable to do without the Munich men Winston did something quite different. He inspired them. He made them work above themselves. He made them work like demons. A right-wing Munich man in eclipse, Sam Hoare, went to Spain to try to stop Franco from entering the war on the German side. Whatever the influence of Hoare was, the declaration of war which Britain expected hourly from Franco did not come. Month followed month and Spain remained neutral. In all-important Washington Lord Lothian, one of the principals of the now-dead Cliveden Set, was bringing to Americans a new and entirely more sympathetic picture of what too many considered an imperialist war. Here a traditional isolationism was in conflict with a new awareness that the world had become too small and tyranny too large for the old comfortable ideas. England watched this soul-searching American quest for her own mission with deep anxiety, for depending on which philosophy prevailed would depend whether England won or lost the war. Franklin D. Roosevelt emerged as England's friend and savior. Lothian became one of England's civilian heroes and when he died Churchill sent Lord Halifax, another Munich man, to replace him, and he became an even better ambassador than Lothian.

America was rarely out of Winston's thoughts. He knew that his speeches were listened to as eagerly in the United States as in Britain and they were angled accordingly. Sometimes he spoke to America directly, as when he appealed for arms: "We shall not fail or falter; we shall not weaken or tire. Neither the shock of battle nor the long-drawn trials of vigilance and exertion will wear us down. Give us the tools and we will finish the job." Always he addressed America inferentially, as when he told the House: "If we stand up to him (Hitler) all Europe may be free and the life of the world may move forward into the broad, sunlit uplands. But if we fail, the whole world, including the United States, including all we have known and cared for, will sink into the abyss of a new Dark Age, made more sinister, and perhaps more protracted, by the lights of

Lord Lothian warns America.

Wide World Photos.

A Nazi bomber over London.

perverted science. Let us therefore brace ourselves that, if the British Empire and its Commonwealth last for a thousand years, men will say, 'This was their finest hour.' " His secretaries have confessed that, in the emotion of the times and the exalted state they all shared, as they took down Churchill's words they choked back tears.

In the fall the Luftwaffe appeared over England and the tiny R.A.F. went up after them in the Spitfires and Hurricanes which were beginning to roll from the factories under the direction of the inspired Beaverbrook. Goering had planned to knock the R.A.F. out as a prior move to invasion, but somehow the Spitfires were still in the sky when a badly bloodied Luftwaffe withdrew to think things over. "Never in the field of human conflict," said Churchill

180

London in Flames.

to the Commons, "was so much owed by so many to so few." After a pause the German planes came again under cover of night with the Blitz that lit London in flames every night for fifty-seven nights.

Responsibility and destiny seemed now to have liberated Winston Churchill's spirit in every way. He had always been brilliant *but*. Now the wretched *but* that had held him from the stars like a mooring rope had been at last cut away and his spirit soared. It was difficult to see in the Prime Minister of England the protesting, sometimes despairing, often defensive, occasionally self-pitying figure of earlier years. Utterly confident of himself he ate, drank and smoked more prodigiously than ever, dressed more outrageously, retiring no matter how black the news to a peaceful and dreamless sleep, then awakening bright-eyed and eager for work.

Under the bombs and far into the night to the approach of dawn Churchill paced the floors at Downing Street, in a pale-blue, one-piece "siren" suit which reminded his colleagues unflatteringly of children's rompers, an effect which was disconcertingly compounded by his round shape and pink cherubic features, with strands of reddish hair sticking up from his bald head. Not even the cigar in his mouth or glass of Scotch or champagne or brandy in his hand could change the impression Churchill gave of an enormous, precocious baby. He indulged his tastes in dress to the full. He often did business in velvet slippers and a dressing gown decorated with green dragons. His Trinity House naval uniform was popular. He occasionally appeared in full-dress uniform of the Army or R.A.F. which he wore with a military assurance and spruceness that was somehow—although it should not have been—unexpected.

Setbacks stimulated rather than depressed him. The allies suffered a serious propaganda blow inside occupied Europe when the Prime Minister of the free Dutch Government in London, de Geer, lost heart and slunk back to Holland via neutral Portugal. His successor, Pieter Gerbrandy, called on Winston who was somewhat moody about the whole affair. Understandably embarrassed the

The Crisis brought forth the Man (sketch by William Sharp).

Dutchman became confused in his English. "Goodbye, Mr. Churchill," he cried heartily as he entered. Winston's unfriendly eyebrows
flew skyward. "What?" he exclaimed. "Going already?"

From Churchill's churning brain flooded schemes, observations,
instructions, ideas. Not all the ideas were good and some were
downright bad. Some of his less successful planning dealt with
what the Government would do if London were invaded and occupied or even knocked out by the Blitz. There were ideas to move
into the country in the case of invasion, and to hold Cabinet meetings in suburban Hampstead if Central London were blown to bits.
The reason the schemes were ineffective, one suspects, was that
the planners themselves were secretly determined not to leave London at all, whatever happened. The King, who like many shy men,
was physically fearless, flatly refused to leave the country in the
event of invasion. In the end the King stayed in Buckingham
Palace (which was bombed), Churchill stayed at Downing Street
(which was bombed), and Parliament stayed at Westminster (which
was also bombed) until the war ended. When a bomb knocked
out the Commons the Members took over the Lords. Churchill
wandered through the rubble of the chambers where his voice had
been heard for so long and ruminated. "We make buildings," he
said, "and they make us."

But most of his ideas were wise and a few breathtaking. He ordered, despite the crying need for defensive weapons, that landing
barges be manufactured and even used in commando raids on the
coast of Europe. This encouraged the British to dream of the day
when they would return to the Continent. Churchill had little ap-
petite for defensive warfare. He was impatient even in these days
when the nation was only half-armed to go on to the offensive. With
an invasion still expected hourly he sent troop reinforcements round
the South African cape to General Wavell in Egypt where a handful of British soldiers were facing the main Italian army who had
moved gingerly across the border into Egypt from Libya. Wavell,

The Prime Minister and Mr. Brendan Bracken inspect the ruins
of the House of Commons.

Churchill with Sergeant Thompson visit the ruined homes and
factories of East London.

without reluctance attacked and, in one of the most astounding victories in the entire history of warfare, destroyed ten Italian divisions,
captured 130,000 men, hundreds of Italian tanks and guns, all with
two divisions and with a loss of 2,000 men.

In London and at the Prime Minister's official country residence
at Chequers, military men, scientists, aides and ministers were
worked day and night, without mercy. Once Churchill's private
detective, Thompson, was withered by a blast of fury and left
Churchill's presence shaken. General Sir Hastings (Pug) Ismay,
Churchill's military adviser, took pity on the unfortunate man. "I
get it just the same, Thompson," he said sympathetically. "If it
lightens the load, it is worth it."

Nothing was too small for the Prime Minister's attention. At
one of the worst periods of the war he sent out (a) a persistent correspondence on whether candy would have to be rationed, (b)

orders that tree-felling operations should keep in consideration the beauty of the English countryside, and (c) that girls in the A.T.S. should be treated kindly and as ladies. Visiting Scapa Flow he examined one of the wooden dummy battleships, exact down to the smallest details, designed to hoodwink German scout planes, and told his escorts that no German would waste a bomb on her.

"But she has not been spotted even by our own reconnaissance," he was told.

"Then they need spectacles," said Churchill. "There are no seagulls about her. You will always find gulls about a living ship. Keep garbage in the water day and night, bow and stern of all these." He smiled a little and added, "Feed the gulls and fool the Germans." This last deliberately trite little maxim reported by the private detective, Thompson, was designed to cheer the men up and make them chortle after his earlier criticism. Churchill knew that his visits were events of the first importance to the fighting men, and criticism to men who saw him so rarely and with such excited anticipation would be a hurtful and abiding wound.

He had the same sense of consideration for soldiers at all formal ceremonies. About inspecting a Guard of Honor he told a colleague, "Look every man straight in the face as you pass him. The sergeant major has had them all standing on parade in a hot sun. . . . If you go by talking to whoever is with you and looking the other way it is pretty flat for the men."

Not least in the conflict between London and Berlin was the trading of insults between Hitler and Churchill, but the gutter-bred Austrian was not in the same league as the descendant of the Dukes of Marlborough. "If we look at our enemies," said Hitler, "we see this gabbler, this drunkard Churchill. What has he done all his life? This hypocritical fellow! This lazybones of the first rank!"

Said Churchill, "This wicked man, the repository and embodiment of many forms of soul-destroying hate, this monstrous product of former wrongs and shame. . . ."

The year 1940 ended with the graph rising at a rate which would have seemed impossible six months earlier. London was battered but cheerful and bombers of the R.A.F. were beginning to hit back almost blow for blow. The British Army was victorious in Africa. The Navy, reinforced by fifty over-age destroyers from America, was fighting off U-Boat attacks on the convoys and holding its own. In the United States following the election for the third time of Franklin Roosevelt, the voice of the anglophile grew progressively louder as the voice of the anglophobe grew fainter. At the close of the year Mussolini, seeking a cheap victory, sent his army from Albania into Greece and was promptly thrown out again by the under-equipped, half-shod, magnificent little Greek Army.

In the Spring of 1941 much that had been gained was lost. General Wavell sent troops he could not spare from Africa to Greece to help England's gallant ally. General Rommel, who had moved to Africa with German soldiers to stiffen the gentle Italians, took advantage of the situation, attacked and drove the British back to the Egyptian border, leaving behind the British outpost of Tobruk which was besieged but held out. The Germans then struck at Greece and Yugoslavia and knocked them both out of the war. England was alone once more, and victory, which had seemed at the beginning of the year to be at least a possibility, now looked farther away than ever.

The Germans had beaten everybody. The strongest adversaries lasted perhaps a week longer than the weakest, but all crumpled before the *blitzkrieg*. The dilemma of the Germans was that at the end of it all they found themselves no nearer to winning the war. All they had was more territory, more occupied populations to control, while the basic problem remained. *Was nun?* What now? On June 22, 1941, Hitler sent the Wehrmacht roaring into the Soviet Union against Stalin's gray Russian masses. The German military machine found itself within a matter of weeks at the gates of Leningrad and Moscow. The Russian soldiers were outfought, the Rus-

Franklin Roosevelt and Winston Churchill after the signing of the Atlantic
Charter, with Admirals King and Leahy and Averill Harriman.

sian generals outgeneraled. It was the old familiar story of repeated
German victory. But the Russians refused to lie down or give in.
They went on fighting. A wave of Russia-adoration swept England.

Through these months of modest victories and serious reverses
England and the United States had grown much closer. England's
resistance, Churchill's speeches, Roosevelt's determination not to let
the other great democracy die, all made possible and even desirable
what would have been unthinkable a year before, a meeting between the heads of the two states. In the fall of 1941 Winston
Churchill and Franklin Roosevelt met in mid-Atlantic for the drawing up of the Atlantic Charter. This was a declaration of the principles of free nations, and a guarantee by the United States and
the British Empire of liberation and freedom to all people oppressed
by Nazism. It was, in effect, a declaration of *moral* war against Hitler's Germany by the United States. The Prime Minister of England and the President of the United States both knew that the

189

winning of the war and perhaps the future of mankind depended on their liking each other. And like each other they did.

The relationship is perhaps best exemplified by the story told by Harry Hopkins, personal assistant to the President, and its aftermath, how Churchill, staying at the White House, emerged pink from the bath to find himself confronted by the President, who had been wheeled into Winston's rooms. Roosevelt began to apologize, but Churchill bowed the apologies away, "The Prime Minister of Great Britain has nothing to conceal," he said, "from the President of the United States."

Churchill was later queried about this by the late Robert E. Sherwood and insisted that he always received the President in at least a bath towel. "I could not possibly have made such a statement," he said chuckling. "The President himself would have been well aware that it was not strictly true."

On December 7, 1941, the world changed forever. The Japanese bombed Pearl Harbor. Declarations of war followed: Japan against Britain and America, America against Japan, Italy and then Germany against America.

With the war suddenly spilled around the globe, everything at first went wrong. The U.S. Fleet was all but destroyed at Pearl Harbor. The Japanese swarmed over Malaya, the Philippines and the South Pacific. The mighty English battleships *Prince of Wales* and *Repulse,* sailing against the Japanese, were sunk within a few minutes of each other, and British confidence in the Fleet which had been unshaken since Nelson's day was given a terrible blow. To make matters worse, Winston Churchill was in the United States when it happened. Soon afterward the great fortress of Singapore fell. Churchill was in the United States again in the summer when Tobruk, the Allied fortress in Libya, now occupied by South Africans, capitulated to the Germans after a shockingly bad performance. He was chatting with Roosevelt when the news came in. The friendship between the two men was never more noble. Roose-

At Casablanca, with Generals Giraud and DeGaulle. The two quarrelling generals did not want to pose together.

velt had no recriminations, only what words he could utter of support and sympathy. Churchill, whose humor stayed with him even at the worst of times, declared himself the unhappiest Englishman in America since Burgoyne.

Bit by bit the news got better. Generals Alexander and Montgomery went to Cairo and led the British Army facing Rommel into attack and routed him utterly at El Alamein. It was brilliant. It was the last triumph of British arms alone. The Russians beat the Germans at Stalingrad and the Americans, under a new and personable general, Dwight D. Eisenhower, with British support, landed in North Africa and reclaimed French Africa for France.

At the conclusion of the campaign Churchill met Roosevelt at Casablanca in French Morocco to decide what kind of a victory they would settle for. The price they put was high. The war would be waged until Germany and Japan surrendered unconditionally to the allies. Immediately on his return to England Winston's tem-

At General Eisenhower's headquarters in Algiers with Anthony Eden, General Sir Alan Brooke, Air Chief Marshal Tedder, Admiral Sir Andrew B. Cunningham, Generals Alexander, Marshall, Eisenhower and Montgomery.

perature rose precipitately and he went down with pneumonia. Raging with resentment he agreed to go to bed. "I call pneumonia the old man's friend," said one of his doctors unsympathetically, "because it takes them off so gently." Winston was not amused. He said something like "Grrrr!" and buried himself in *Moll Flanders*.

The year 1943 was marked by the invasion of Sicily and Italy—Churchill flew back to North Africa in June to help with the plans—by the collapse of Mussolini's Fascist regime, and the unexpectedly hard slog up the mountainous back of the Italian peninsula with the long and costly holdup at Monte Cassino. The monastery at the top—one of Catholicism's noblest shrines after the Vatican itself—was destroyed by American bombers, but even then Alexander's mixed force of Americans, Canadians, British, New Zealanders, Indians and Poles could not move the Germans from the slopes. Churchill dreaded that the war which up to now had been a war of movement, would bog down into a slugging match as had happened in the trenches of the first World War. His messages to General Alexander began to assume a most uncharacteristic note of querulousness.

"I wish you would explain to me," he said once, "why this passage by Cassino, Monastery Hill, etc., all on a front of two or three miles, is the only place which you must keep butting at. About five or six divisions have been worn out going into these jaws. Of course I do not know the ground or the battle conditions, but looking at it from afar it is puzzling why . . . no attacks can be made on the flanks. . . ."

To break the deadlock he supported the plan for a flank landing above the German lines at Anzio near Rome, which was not a success.

The burden which Churchill bore, once so stimulating, took on a new arduousness, and his Cabinet too seemed to lose something of their zip. Winston's son, Randolph, dropped into German-occupied Yugoslavia to serve with Tito's partisans. Leo Amery's son, Julian, was doing the same job in Albania. Lord Beaverbrook's son, young Max Aitken, had won the D.F.C. as a Battle of Britain pilot and subsequently added to it the D.S.O. As if the Cabinet ministers had not enough weight of responsibility, they must also have had in their minds the fear that they would lose their sons in combat.

At home Winston had to put up with General de Gaulle, hypersensitive for the fair name of France and his own position as the symbol of fighting France. This was all very well except that fighting France seemed to be busier fighting Americans and British in the conference rooms than Germans in the field. De Gaulle, operating from London, was noncooperative to his friends and allies, finding everywhere elusive insults to his national and personal *amour propre*. It is possible that de Gaulle was pursuing some mysterious and sinister policies of his own because Churchill ordered papers to be prepared listing his "misdeeds" and showed them to Duff

Cooper after an argument in which he accused Duff Cooper of being too pro-de Gaulle. Duff Cooper read the papers impressed, and admitted in his memoirs that they were a "grave indictment."

Churchill's troubles with de Gaulle were nothing compared to his troubles with Stalin. Winston had undertaken the onerous job of liaison between Roosevelt and Stalin, flying back and forth between Moscow and Washington. Stalin had demanded a second front in 1942 and 1943. When none arrived except for the disappointing campaign in Italy, Stalin insulted Winston roundly. The losses to British ships in the convoys to Murmansk were dismissed contemptuously. "The Royal Navy is frightened," Stalin jeered. "It turns back half way."

Once they had a row in public in the middle of a banquet in Moscow, witnessed by Churchill's private detective, Thompson. Churchill had told the interpreter Pavlov to suggest that he (Churchill) and Stalin withdraw for a private conference and that it had better be soon because he was leaving on schedule whether anything was accomplished or not. "He stuck his finger," said Thompson admiringly, "right in Joe Stalin's belly." Next morning the Prime Minister was respectfully informed that Marshal Stalin was most anxious to have a private visit with Mr. Churchill and would he be so kind as to etc., etc.

No one has yet tried to estimate what it cost Winston in pride to run back and forth between Stalin and Roosevelt. Only the magnanimity of his spirit can explain why Winston, never slow with a riposte and never noticeably reluctant to fight anyone at any time, endured so much discourtesy and rudeness from Stalin. He never forgot the sufferings of the Russian people and their huge losses. There may have been another reason. The Communists were never slow to threaten a separate peace with Hitler if their demands were not met.

Still Winston could never be repressed for long. He came back from America wearing a cowboy Stetson and from Russia with a

194

UPI.

Winston and Stalin.

Cossack fur hat. The American generals and politicians had never seen anything like him. Once, in England, Mark Clark, an awed observer, watched blankly while Churchill rose from a conference table to rub his back against the wall. "I guess I got them in Egypt," he exclaimed cheerfully. "His enthusiasm," said Clark, "extended to his eating. When soup was put before him he tackled it vigorously, his mouth about two inches from the liquid and his shoulders hunched over. He ate with a purring and a slurping and the spoon went from bowl to mouth so rapidly you could hardly see it until he scraped the bottom, and bawled 'More soup!' Turning to his guests he would say, 'Good soup, ain't it?' "

General Marshall staggered, white as a sheet, from a conference with Churchill that did not end until 2:45 A.M. General Alan Brooke watched him go with a smile. "I wonder how he would have liked to work permanently with Winston," he said, "and be kept out of bed three or four nights a week."

Even Winston was weakening. He was far from well when he left England by ship in November 1943 for the series of conferences which was to end in the Teheran Conference of the Big Three, Churchill, Roosevelt and Stalin. He stopped first in Cairo to see Roosevelt, and to meet Chiang Kai Shek and Madame Chiang. He chafed impatiently through days of talks with the Chinese at the Mena House Hotel opposite the Pyramids. He wanted to get down to serious talks with Roosevelt about how they should tackle Stalin, and once or twice suggested that their Chinese colleagues make a tour of the Pyramids and enjoy themselves but without success. He noticed skeptically the awe and admiration in which Chiang Kai Shek was held by the Americans. He found he liked both Chiang and his wife, but by Chiang's overall record against the Japanese he was not impressed.

By the time he reached Teheran he had lost his voice completely. Teheran was a tremendous propaganda move bringing the three statesmen together, and it hit German morale hard. At Teheran

The Fates Decide

Stalin joined Winston and Roosevelt in the policy of "unconditional surrender," but their unity was more apparent than real. On the way home Winston had planned to visit Alexander at his Italian HQ but his condition grew steadily worse. General Eisenhower met him when he landed at Tunis and was startled at his appearance. Churchill was to stay overnight at Ike's house and the general asked him what was wrong. "I am afraid I shall have to stay with you longer than I planned," said Winston apologetically and feebly. "I am completely at the end of my tether and I cannot go to the front until I have recovered some of my strength." He then collapsed in bed and almost died. For a while he was delirious. "The ruins of ancient Carthage," he mumbled. "The sound of the Romans and Hasdrubal . . . What better place can I die than here." His physicians, Lord Moran and Dr. Bedford were rushed to his side armed with the medical miracle of the time, M. and B. From the depths of the pillows came a weak Churchillian chuckle. "M. and B., Moran and Bedford." He recovered.

On June 6, 1944, the great day came—D-Day—and the Americans and British landed on French soil. At first the forces were more or less equal in numbers, but very soon the Americans far outnumbered the others, with the First, Third, Seventh and Ninth Armies ashore and the Fifteenth on the way, against England's solitary Second Army, Canada's First Army and the French First, a patchwork though dashing affair. In the field the British soldiers fought less well than before. While the Americans broke through and sped across the French countryside the British were pinned down by German armor at Caen. With the Germans on the run, British paratroopers were dropped to cut off their retreat at Arnhem in Holland. It was a bad tactic. They were too far ahead for any link-up to be practical. The Germans rallied and overwhelmed them after a furious and gallant struggle. It was a brave battle, but it was also the solitary defeat suffered by the Allies in a year of constant victory, and it was the British who suffered it.

Keystone Press Agency.

A few days after D-day Churchill visits General Eisenhower in Normandy.

Something had happened to the British; it was something that neither Winston Churchill, nor the British, nor God could do anything about. Even as the war had changed in Britain's favor and victory was in sight, disillusion began to spread more and more widely. England had spent one glorious year as the symbol of freedom and the English had enjoyed it. It suited their temperament. England had done more than hang on. She had started to win. The R.A.F. had beaten the Luftwaffe. The British Eighth Army had beaten the unbeatable Rommel and his Afrika Korps. At the same time English convoys had supplied the Russians with arms that may have meant the difference between defeat and survival to their ally and with the back of her hand England had knocked Italy out of the war. It was, by any standards, a great record and the hangover that followed it was a painful one.

England had gone to bed one night the bastion of liberty and she had woken up next morning, still brushing the sleep from her eyes, to find herself a second-class power, fighting the war on sufferance between her two big allies. When the Russians and the Americans had taken over the war England's sense of identification faded and the symbol was lost.

It was the liberated people themselves, their minds made vivid by suffering and oppression who felt the change most keenly. There had been a time when London, blitzed and indomitable, had been the symbol of hope to them. They lived by the broadcasts of the B.B.C. The entry of Russia and America redirected their aspirations. It was noticeable and sometimes startling to see. When British troops liberated a village in France or Italy they were politely cheered, but the crowds were somehow disappointed. It was the legendary Americans they wanted to see. The G.I.'s were hysterically garlanded with flowers, champagne, girls. Soldiers other than the ever-cheerful British Tommy would have found it sobering.

True, Roosevelt remained Winston's friend, but the President was a sick man now and in his illness he was showing streaks of vanity

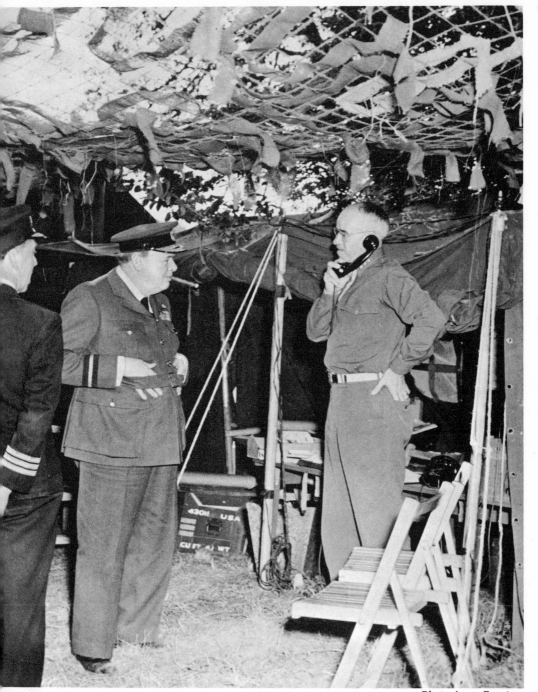

In August, 1944, Churchill visits Lt. Gen. Omar N. Bradley in France,
waiting patiently as Gen. Bradley issues orders to officers
of his command over a field telephone.

that served Churchill badly. He talked constantly of "Imperialism" and "colonialism," urged Winston to give Hong Kong back to China as a gesture. His distrust of Winston affected the other American chiefs. When Winston urged Eisenhower to drive on to Vienna, the Commander resisted. "I felt that the Prime Minister's real concern," said Ike, "was possibly of a political rather than a military nature." Vienna was ultimately occupied by the Russians.

The first major notes of ugly discord sounded in the winter of 1944. While the Russians were sweeping through Eastern Europe British troops liberated Greece, which had been under German occupation for four years. Immediately the Greek Communist underground attempted a *coup d'état*. Greeks who should have been fighting the Germans started to fight each other. Winston ordered the British to support the legitimate Government and help suppress the Communist rising. There was an uproar in the United States. Stalin, they said, will be furious. "British Imperialism" was at work again, fighting for Greek monarchy against the "people." Hopkins cabled Churchill angrily, "I must confess I am greatly disturbed by this turn of events . . . at a time when the battle is joined in Europe and Asia and all our energy is required for the defeat of the enemy . . ." Nevertheless, Greece alone of the East European states was liberated by a western country and did not go Communist, thanks to Churchill. He flew to Athens at the height of the battle when snipers were still shooting from the rooftops. It was Christmas Eve, 1944, and Winston had just turned seventy. This did not save him from the kicks. Americans were enjoying their friendship with the Russians too much to want it imperiled by that wicked old English Imperialist. "We find the Russians easy people to deal with," said Harry Hopkins. "The Russians undoubtedly like the American people. They trust the United States more than any other power in the world" (especially more than England is the unspoken inference). And General Eisenhower wrote, "In his generous instincts, in his love of laughter, in his devotion to a comrade,

The Yalta Conference.

and in his healthy, direct outlook on the affairs of workaday life, the ordinary Russian seems to me to bear a marked similarity to what we call 'an average American' " (which nobody could say about the British!).

The Big Three met for the second time at Yalta in January, 1945. This was to be the conference to decide the future of the world from which the Japanese and German menaces had been removed. Churchill was in that most unenviable of positions, the third person sitting in on a love affair. Stalin and Roosevelt realized that the important thing was to win the other over to his side. Churchill could be taken for granted. They even combined to needle Churchill in terms that, though friendly, had a distinctly sharp point. Churchill growled back that he was constantly being "beaten up" as a reactionary but he was the only one of the three who could be thrown out of office tomorrow. Stalin sneered that he was scared of what would happen at the next British election. Churchill replied quickly that he was proud of the right of the British to throw their government out whenever they felt like it. Roosevelt seems to have said nothing at this exchange.

Around the marginal and largely insignificant agreements reached at Yalta a vast and controversial literature has arisen. Suffice it here to say that Churchill had the least to say of any of the three on the decisions reached. By now the Russians, Americans and British stood on the borders of Nazi Germany. The Third Reich, which Hitler had boasted would last for a thousand years, was at its last gasp, its youth all but wiped out, its cities a desolate rubble from air attack, its philosophy drained by a decade of shame into a blank despairing nihilism. In the Spring of 1945 came the last great squeeze. Churchill urged that the Anglo-American forces rush headlong for Berlin, and capture this great symbolic prize. Eisenhower dismissed the idea and soon Berlin was surrounded by the Russians.

On April 25, 1945, at Torgau in the heart of Germany, American GIs and Russian soldiers joined hands. The Yanks, fed for three years on propaganda about their loyal, suffering, Tolstoyan allies, were surprised and repelled by their comrades' backwardness and naive savagery. A week later Nazi Germany expired. Victory in Europe was utter and unconditional.

But Roosevelt had not lived to see it. He had died on April 12, taken by the weight of his heavy cross, on the eve of victory. The enemies were dead too. Mussolini had been shot by Italian partisans and strung by his heels with his mistress in a garage on the Piazza Caretta, Milan, while the people spat on him. Hitler took his own life in the depths of his bunker in the besieged rubble of Berlin while the Russian boots thumped almost over his head. Winston Churchill led his Cabinet to prayer in Westminster Abbey and then prepared to face an immediate general election in Britain. Stalin

V E Day.

alone remained, supreme in his Moscow fastness. Peace was in his hands to mold, and he was answerable to no one.

Churchill did not perhaps foresee the future as clearly as is sometimes asserted by his right-wing idolators in the United States seeking a stick to beat Roosevelt. He realized the necessity for a continuing friendship with Russia, but he also saw the dangers more clearly than Roosevelt, or, for that matter, Stalin. Can anyone doubt that had Churchill possessed the power of Roosevelt or Stalin, with the divisions and the gold, the peace would have been a more efficient one, and the world today a safer one?

Part VI

The Bright Twilight

Crowds surround Churchill's car in Coventry on June 29, 1945
at the start of his thousand mile election tour.

6

The Bright Twilight

THE BRITISH ELECTION WAS SET FOR JULY, 1945. THE PRIME MIN-
ister, campaigning enthusiastically, beaming and giving the V-sign,
seemed supreme, irresistible, utterly confident.

True, now that the dust of battle had settled and the four-year
political truce had ended, the Tories stood naked before the electorate as the party of Munich which had gotten the nation into the
mess in the first place, while the Socialists appeared to be the party
of the future, the party which would provide the "homes for heroes"
which Lloyd George had promised the returning soldiers in 1919
and had not delivered.

Incomprehensibly Winston had failed to read the signs. As far
back as D-Day there was an incident that might have shattered
some of his illusions had he chosen to interpret it correctly. He and
Ernest Bevin were watching a line of British troops embarking for
Europe. Excitement was in the air. In every mind was the thought
that this operation was going to win the war, and afterward the soldiers could go home. As they saw the two great figures of wartime
England standing there the soldiers cheered, and one shouted, "See
they don't let us down when we come back this time, Ernie!"

Ernie? Why not Winston? Who was meant by "they"? The fact
was that the British Tommy had a blistering hatred of everything
that had to do with the Tory Party. He had no intention of voting
for it under any circumstances, under no matter what leader it presented itself. The figure of Churchill tended consequently to be an
irritant. He confused the issue for the soldier who preferred to see
everything as deep Tory black and spotless Labor white.

209

Back to London, in early July, from his brilliant campaign against the Japanese in Burma came General Sir William Slim, and he called on the Prime Minister, who was in fine campaign fettle. Winston asked Slim how he thought his soldiers would vote. Slim was a tough man who did not mince words. "Seventy per cent will vote Labor, sir," he said.

Winston was surprised. "What will the other thirty do?"

"They will abstain from voting at all, sir, out of affection for you."

At election meetings the scenes were stormy and Tory candidates were drowned out by hecklers. Rocks were thrown through windows displaying Tory posters. Clement Attlee, leader of the Labor Party, based his campaign on the nationalization of the mines, the railroads, the Bank of England, the cable and wireless services, medicine, steel. Against these far-reaching and exciting proposals the Tories seemed to be campaigning, as a cynic remarked, with nothing more than a picture of Winston Churchill.

A few days before the election Winston left for Potsdam, near Berlin, for a Big Three meeting to agree on the administration of a smitten, broken Germany. But the Big Three were changed now. The world had grown accustomed to the old war leaders together: Stalin, extravagantly epauletted, beaming, his eyes like slits; Winston, hunched and smiling half to himself as though he were enjoying some secret joke; Roosevelt, his head flung challengingly back. Nothing symbolized the beginning of a new era more than the sight of the almost unknown figure who had replaced Roosevelt, the spruce little man in a double-breasted suit with a smile a little too bright and a little too wide to suggest confidence. The world was moving forward from the familiar into the profound unknown of the postwar.

Winston, back in London for the election, awoke on election morning with a stab and a premonition that "the power to shape the future would be denied me." The election returns showed the same picture everywhere, a landslide victory for the Socialists. The Labor Party captured 393 seats, the Tories 189, assorted Liberals 25.

Potsdam.

Courtesy of the News Chronicle, London.

The Communists, who had campaigned across the country on the strength of Russia's popularity, doubled their representation in the House, from one to two.

There is no delay in English politics, only the shortest interim period between election and inauguration. Winston hurried to the Palace to hand in his resignation to King George VI. "The verdict of the electors had been so overwhelmingly expressed," he said, "that I did not wish to remain even for an hour responsible for their affairs." Clement Attlee went to Potsdam as Prime Minister to join Stalin and Truman.

Britons expected now that Winston would retire to paint pictures, write books and give the world the benefit of his wisdom as elder statesman. He was seventy years old at the time of his election defeat. In fact he was about to embark on his most furious period of activity.

He had been the first to see that the wartime alliance was being deliberately killed by Stalin, who had no intention of allowing the democratic winds of his western friends to blow across his brooding empire. Franklin Roosevelt, in his last days, had been growing increasingly anxious about Stalin's attitude, but now only Winston was left to give expression to that fear. Only he understood it. The rest of the United States and Britain still lived in a rosy glow. The United Nations Organization had been formed on the basis of the Atlantic Charter. Stalin was still "Uncle Joe," the Russians still their friends and allies, "easy to get on with" like "average Americans." Winston resolved on a last plea to Stalin, and sent him a telegram:

"There is not much comfort in looking on to a future where you and the countries you dominate, plus the Communist parties in many other States are all drawn up on one side and those who rally to the English-speaking nations and their associates or Dominions are on the other. It is quite obvious that their quarrel would tear the world to pieces and that all us leading men on either side who had anything to do with that would be shamed before history. Even embarking on a long period of suspicions, of abuse and counterabuse of opposing policies would be a disaster hampering the great de-

Anti-Churchill demonstration on Park Avenue. New York, 1946.

velopments of world prosperity for the masses which are attainable only through our trinity."

There was no response from Stalin, and Winston determined to awaken the world, and particularly the United States, to the danger they were facing. Westminster College in Fulton, Missouri, had given him an honorary degree and he decided this would be a good opportunity to utter his warning. President Truman, who was learning fast, went along to hear his famous speech denouncing Russia in which the expression "Iron Curtain" was used for the first time and in which he warned that it would be "criminal madness" to give away the secret of the atom bomb—then possessed only by the United States.

Winston's reception was cool. Just as the British did not wish to hear Churchill's truths about Nazi Germany in 1934, so the American people did not wish to hear unpalatable facts about the Russians in 1946. The American press was polite; Winston was in a way an honorary American property. It smiled tolerantly that the warrior was giving himself nightmares. Pearl Buck said, "We are nearer war tonight than last night." Young American Communists staged a demonstration, wielding witty slogans like, "Send this bundle back to Britain" and chanting, "Winnie, Winnie, go away. U-N-O has come to stay."

It was clear that Winston had no intention of fading away. For the next six years as the head of a Tory Party demoralized and in impotent minority he was to do battle with enthusiasm against the massed ranks of the Socialists opposite. But there was nothing he could do to stop the nationalization of the coal mines and the Bank of England and the cable and wireless companies. India was freed, and the great disengagement of England from her empire began. The war had given the Socialist politicians experience of high office within the Coalition. They were far from being newcomers to power, and they possessed both skill and arrogance.

Clement Attlee, a steely and imperturbable man but capable of both warmth and wit, was a much stronger Prime Minister than Conservative jokers made out. As *Time* magazine once put it, "Attlee could walk with Dante through Hell and emerge remarking that different people had different tastes, but it did seem rather too hot."

Sir Stafford Cripps, wealthy lawyer, a vegetarian not through conviction but from poor health, was Minister of Economic Affairs. Winston admired his intellect but otherwise had little affection for him. In the House in 1946 he said of Cripps, "Neither of his colleagues can compare with him in the acuteness and energy of mind with which he devotes himself to so many topics injurious to the strength and welfare of the State." In private Winston is said to have declared, "There but for the grace of God goes God," and there were times when he seemed to have difficulty in pronouncing the name, which came out sounding something like "Sir Stifford Crapps."

And Aneurin Bevan. It is said that when Bevan arrived at the House fresh from Wales Lloyd George took him under his wing and advised him to ignore the little fellows, attack the big ones. So Bevan attacked Lloyd George. No one then present will ever forget the scene in the Commons when Bevan launched into an attack on the Communists and the Soviet Union with an impact that was nothing short of crushing. The two Communist members writhed and squeaked, "Cheapskate!" in voices growing progressively feebler. Almost at the end Bevan lost his thread and automatically, it seemed, found himself attacking Churchill instead. Winston leaned forward and said something which was inaudible to all but a few. What he said was, "Don't spoil a good speech." Bevan stopped, stammered, resumed the thread and went off again without another reference to Churchill.

Ernest Bevin tangled as frequently with Winston, but they never forgot the debt they owed to each other. At six o'clock one morning in September, 1947, Bevin was awakened by a telephone call from New York which stated that Andrei Vishinsky of Russia had attacked Winston Churchill in the U.N. and called him "as bad as Hitler." Bevin hurried from his bed, called an early morning conference of Foreign Office officials and drafted a reply for the British delegate to make. The draft stated, among other things, that Mr. Churchill had done more to fight Fascism than any Communist in the world, that he had worked in London while German planes, fueled with Soviet oil, were shoveling bombs on the capital.

Winston could not win. The majority against him was too large in confidence and the minority he led, too flaccid. Once when he ran out of argument he startled the Socialists by putting his tongue out at them. Perhaps he should have retired, but the Tories would have been a drab lot without him. Anthony Eden was his chosen successor, but he had none of Winston's eloquence and pugnacity. And Winston enjoyed himself. "When I want to tease Anthony," he chuckled, "I remind him that Mr. Gladstone formed his last administration at the age of eighty-three."

The full-time job of remaking a beaten and dispirited party represented only a tiny fraction of Winston's endeavors in this bright twilight period of his life. Beginning in 1948 the six majestic volumes on *The Second World War* appeared one by one. Each had

Courtesy of the *Daily Express*, London.

Churchill working on *The Second World War* in his study at Chartwell.

a special theme. The first, *The Gathering Storm*, told "How the English-speaking peoples through their unwisdom, carelessness and good nature allowed the wicked to rearm." The second, *Their Finest Hour,* told "How the British people held the fort ALONE till those who had been half blind were half ready." The third, *The Grand Alliance,* "How the British fought on with Hardship their Garment until Soviet Russia and the United States were drawn into the Great Conflict." The fourth, *The Hinge of Fate,* "How the power of the Grand Alliance became predominant." The fifth, *Closing the Ring,* "How Nazi Germany was isolated and assailed on All Sides." And the sixth and last, *Triumph and Tragedy,* tells with a stinging pain "How the great democracies triumphed and so were able to resume the follies which had so nearly cost them their life."

The moral of the whole work was, "In War, Resolution; In Defeat, Defiance; In Victory, Magnanimity; In Peace, Good Will." These books form the central core around which any fresh history of the second World War has to be built. Translated into innumerable languages they also won for Churchill a Nobel Prize for Literature. One of the most impressive themes of the book was his unfailing loyalty to President Roosevelt, even though with the death of the President his relationship with the family had all but ceased. Winston had received several pinpricks from the Roosevelts. Elliott had brought out a book of Memoirs and private conversations with his father, which made it seem sometimes that Roosevelt considered Winston a bigger menace to the world than Stalin. Even during the war Mrs. Roosevelt had invited the writer Louis Adamic to meet Churchill at dinner, and Adamic had responded to this courtesy with a book called *Dinner at the White House* which was a scurrilous and personal attack on everything the Prime Minister did, said, or represented to the writer. Churchill, annoyed, sued, and the book was withdrawn. After the war the French diplomat, Jacques Dumaine heard him refer to the Roosevelts as "the wicked family of my great friend."

It took a team of eight secretaries, several personal servants, and innumerable honorary aides to keep up with Winston's demands. Many staggered exhausted from his employ too punch drunk to do more than gasp out their memoirs to ghost writers.

Friends and colleagues were likely to be called at any hour of the day or night. There is a well-known Churchill story which has been told in several different forms, probably because it must have happened many times in one form or another. This version takes place at five o'clock in the afternoon with Churchill on the telephone to Lord Ismay, "Pug, I'm having difficulty over my chapter on Syria. I am not quite sure of the sequence of events. I shall be grateful if you can let me have a short memorandum, about 2,000 words. I should like it by ten o'clock tonight."

Ismay is apologetic. "I am afraid ten will be difficult, sir. There is a big dinner tonight at which I have to make a speech."

"That's quite all right, my dear Pug," says Churchill. "There's no urgency in the matter. Ten o'clock tomorrow morning will do just as well."

Not even politics and literature combined satisfied his vast energy. He purchased five hundred acres of land around Chartwell and began serious farming. At the same time he developed a strong desire to own a racing stable. He acquired a gray three-year-old, Colonist II, which started off with a win at Ascot in 1949, went on to win £13,000 in prize money for his master. The pleasure this gave Winston can be imagined. He had taken his father's racing colors, chocolate and pink, as his own and Churchill must in his mind's eye have seen that stern little mustached figure as the colors flashed past the winning post.

In the weighing room Winston was as wide-eyed as a child, watching everything. "This is something new for me," he explained. In 1952 he had five horses in training—Pol Roger, Loving Cup, Non-Stop, Gibraltar III and Prince Arthur—and all of them won races.

He worked at painting with furious concentration, sometimes from early morning until late in the afternoon, sitting there in his siren suit and sombrero, hunched like an enormous egg, put out only if

Winston and Colonist II.

Whenever he could, Winston escaped from English winters. He
particularly loved to paint in the south of France and Italy.

"Sea near Genoa," painted by Winston Churchill.

someone whistled or was bold enough to try looking over his shoulder. As color splashed on color he would mutter to himself the sense of some future speech he planned to give or the sequence of some future literary work. The paintings gathered and overflowed. They hung on the walls at Chartwell and stood in piles in spare rooms, for he made it a principle that none was to be offered for sale. Every year at least one of his pictures was hung in the Royal Academy and as he had begun by submitting his work under the name of "Mr. Winter" it could not be said that his illustrious name had influenced the committee.

But he never stopped working for the return of the Tory Party. As he had done throughout his life he continued to identify himself with Britain's fortunes, and the country's position in the world was a desperate one. All the wealth she possessed in 1914 had been dispersed in two great wars, and she was in debt to the world. First an American loan, and then the Marshall Plan came to her rescue, and little by little the United States was drawn in to hold the outposts that England was surrendering. This clearly was no time for daring and expensive sociological experiments, but Attlee's Labor Party refused to relax one jot of their nationalization programs. They were driven forward by a ghost, the ghost of Ramsay MacDonald, the most detested figure in the British Labor movement. MacDonald had died in 1937, bitter and discredited. Twice he had been Prime Minister and each time he had reneged on Socialist promises with his policy of "Socialism, but not now." Socialists could not bring themselves to repeat such a loathsome slogan, even though there was legitimate excuse for it. They pressed doggedly on with their program, saddling the country with a far greater load of cost and administration than she could bear. As the years passed, Winston's good humor faded and his voice deepened.

"In these last four lavish years," he said in 1949, "the Socialist Government have exacted upwards of £16 thousand millions and spent them—over four times as much every year as was the cost of running the country in our richer days before the war. They have used up every national asset or reserve upon which they could lay their hands; they have taken forty per cent of the national income for the purposes of governmental administration. Our taxation has been the highest in the world. Large incomes are virtually confiscated. . . . The exertions and rewards of the most active class of wage earners and craftsmen have been burdened in times of peace by the harsh direct taxation which in war, when we were fighting for life, may be a matter of pride to bear, but which in victory is at least a disappointment. . . . As has been well said, we ate the Argentine Railways—£110 millions last year as a mere side dish. . . . We have been given or loaned—and have spent—above £1750 thousand mil-

lions by the United States. We have been helped to the extent of
£300 million by Canada, Australia and New Zealand. In all history
no community has ever been helped and kept by gratuitous overseas
aid, that is to say, by the labor of other hard-working peoples, to anything approaching the degree which we have been under the present
Socialist Government."

Shortly after he made this speech, Sir Stafford Cripps devalued
the pound from $4.00 to $2.80, and shortly after that Winston
Churchill celebrated his seventy-fifth birthday. Congratulations
came in from friends and enemies alike. Nothing, perhaps, put England's feelings toward Churchill more perfectly than Low's cartoon
on that occasion. It showed two Churchills, one magnificent with
one hand on a pile of books, his other on a sword, and near him his
painting palette and brushes. It was labeled, "Dear old Winston, the
Nation's pride." The other Churchill was labeled, "Winston,
Naughty Old Party Politician." An average British citizen was push-
ing the second away and crying, "Stand aside, sir. Not even you
will stop me paying my respects."

225

Still the Socialists drove ahead. No party had been so faithful to its pledges and to the trust placed in it by the working classes. But somehow England did not change. The class system still prevailed. Having done everything they had promised and found at the end that almost nothing had changed, the Socialists ran out of ideas and withered away. They fought the elections of 1950 a weary party and squeezed in by six votes. Their leaders were exhausted. Bevin died in April, 1951, a month after his seventieth birthday. Cripps was dying. Attlee and Morrison were sick men. And at the other side of the world another huge crisis was exploding as North Korean Communists swarmed over the thirty-eighth parallel in what was to be the beginning of a new and brutal war. No Parliament could survive so stalemated at home and with such dire threats to security abroad, and in 1951, after the nationalization of steel had been pushed through, the choice was put to the country again.

Despite the stupendous achievements of his life, a life that needed no alterations or erasures, Churchill was vulnerable on one point that rankled in his heart—the allegation that he was a warmonger. It was a charge easier to level than to define. Some of his opponents still brought up "the Dardanelles" to prove their case, which automatically disproved it, for the Gallipoli campaign was intended to "open the war out" and end the blood bath on the Western Front. Others cited Churchill's intervention in Russia. Others said, "Chanak," others, "Antwerp."

In 1951, as Britain went into her third postwar election, "warmonger" was the word that the Socialists were throwing at Churchill. The Korean War was at its bewildering peak of intensity and it seemed that the strife-tired world hung in the balance between cold war and all-out nuclear war. Churchill—like Attlee—was declaring for rearmament, but the old trades union suspicion was concentrated on Churchill. Who in the world would ever think of Attlee as a warmonger? The left-wing London *Daily Mirror*, perhaps the most influential organ of its kind in the world, ran a headline, "WHOSE

Daily Mirror

THURS OCT 25 1951

1½d

FORWARD WITH THE PEOPLE

WHOSE FINGER?

BIG ISSUES OF 1951

Today YOUR finger is on the trigger

SEE YOU DEFEND

PEACE with SECURITY and PROGRESS with FAIR SHARES

VOTE FOR THE PARTY YOU CAN REALLY TRUST

The 'Daily Mirror' believes that Party is Labour

FINGER DO YOU WANT ON THE TRIGGER WHEN THE WORLD SITUATION IS SO DELICATE? Churchill's or Attlee's?"

In vain Churchill fought against the charges and insinuations. "I do not hold that we rearm to fight," he said doggedly. "I hold that we should rearm to parley." On polling day the *Daily Mirror*, with a positively diabolical sense of timing, repeated the headline, and a furious Churchill issued a writ for libel. It was too late. The people took the idea with them to the booths. The big majority the Tories expected did not materialize. The Tories won 323 seats against the Socialists' 295, enough to govern but not nearly enough for comfort. The traditional pendulum of politics had stuck. After six years of Socialism, of wasteful government, declining wealth, high taxation and persistent rationing and austerity, the best the Conservatives could muster was a majority of a score. Many Tories felt that this would be the last Conservative government in their time, a brief pause before a new and even greater swing back to Socialism. One minister said grimly, "The only way we can make it is by being the best damned administration England has ever had." But he said it in a way that suggested he was not too hopeful.

Even so the old man was back, seventy-seven and giving the V-sign from Downing Street just as he had done a decade earlier. Few governments could have been formed with a morale so low and nothing in the first few months of Churchill's administration gave reason for optimism. The economic situation inherited from the Socialists was going through one of its periodic crises, with gold and dollar reserves tumbling. Churchill's attitude seemed out-of-touch and archaic. His first move was to cut his ministers' salaries 20 per cent, a saving of some £30,000, until the economic crisis ended, but this typically aristocratic gesture was not in accord with egalitarian times. He aroused little enthusiasm by trying to get his old wartime staff back and his wartime system of command resumed. Even Churchill's V-sign seemed anachronistic.

Outside the South Kensington polling station.

In the House the Tory ministers were nervous and uncertain. The Socialists began counting the months back to office. Then the Korean War ended. Trade steadied. The prices of the raw materials which England had to import went down and at the same time the demand for her exports increased. The economic drain was stopped and England's financial reserves mounted. The food situation, one of the principal sources of British discontent, eased, and the rationing which had been in force for thirteen years was all but abolished.

Suddenly the sun came out and the country found itself with a successful and confident government. Ministers who had been silent under the jeers of the Socialists found voice in the new spring air, smiled, quipped, and flicked the Opposition like lion tamers baiting lions. There were still complaints about the Prime Minister—after all he was approaching eighty—and some reports said that he was forgetful and eccentric in Cabinet meetings and his age rankled with the younger and more ambitious ministers. Many grumbled openly, but not in his presence! Winston, if he was aware of the discontent, was undisturbed by it. In fact he often seemed to be threatening his friends with his own immortality. A news cameraman taking his picture called out, "I shall photograph you on your hundredth birthday, sir!"

Winston humphed. "I see no reason why you shouldn't, young man. You look healthy enough."

Shortly after Churchill's second administration began England's great King George VI died, killed by overwork and duty. A beautiful new Queen, Elizabeth II, came to the throne, able to benefit early in her reign from the advice of the nation's greatest statesman who, as a young subaltern, had toasted the health of her great-great-grandmother, Queen Victoria. In honor of the Coronation of 1953 he accepted from the Queen the Order of the Garter he had so long refused. Many were rather sorry to see "Mr. Churchill," with all the stark simplicity those two words had meant to so many Englishmen for so long, withdrawn in favor of a lily-gilding "Sir Winston." Mr.

Queen Elizabeth with Winston Churchill and the Canadian
Prime Minister, Mr. St. Laurent.

Sir Winston Churchill leads the procession to the Chapel at Windsor Castle
where he was installed as a Knight of the Garter.

Churchill had claimed all the deference a people could give. Sir
Winston could get no more. In fact the title has shown no more disposition to stick than the name of New York's Avenue of the Americas, which so obstinately remains "Sixth Avenue." Sir Winston
remains Mr. Churchill.

In 1953 the strain of the Coronation told on Churchill and he
went down with a severe stroke which paralyzed him down one side
and kept him out of the Commons for four months. He was given
a great reception on his return, and the Socialists gallantly declared
that "the House had been a duller place in his absence."

Churchill's eightieth birthday, in November, 1954, was a tremendous occasion. Lords and Commons gathered in Westminster
Hall to do him honor. Clement Attlee affirmed he came "not to bury
Caesar but to praise him." He recalled old days. He remembered
when he himself was fighting in the Dardanelles as a captain and
called it "the only imaginative strategic concept of the war." Church-

Photograph by Toni Frissell. Central Office of Information.

Three generations of Churchills at Downing Street after the Coronation.

ill rose, slowly now with his years, and his listeners were seized by that old tingling of the senses which they used to feel while waiting for him to speak during the dark days of the war. They were not disappointed. "I have never accepted," he said modestly, his S's slurring in the old way, "what many people have kindly said, namely that I inspired the nation. Their will was resolute and remorseless, and, as it proved, unconquerable. It fell to me to express it and if I found the right words you must remember that I have always earned my living by my pen and by my tongue. It was the nation and the race dwelling all round the globe that had the lion's heart. I . . ."—and now the great Churchillian boom was heard again with the resounding echo of 1940—"had the luck to be called on to give the r-o-a-r."

There was one false note. The distinguished portrait painter, Graham Sutherland, was commissioned to paint Churchill for the occasion. It was a clever but inappropriate picture in mustards and purples, showing Churchill powerful but gluey-eyed and senile. "It is disgusting," said a Tory leader flatly. Churchill was politely ironic, but hurt. "A remarkable example of modern art," he said. Aneurin Bevan, Winston's old enemy, purred, "a beautiful work."

Still he remained in office declaring to recalcitrant young Conservatives, "It is not because of my love of power for office. I have had an ample share of both. . . . I have the feeling I may, through things that have happened, have an influence on what I care about above all else—the building of a sure and lasting peace."

What he was thinking about was the apparent thaw that had taken place in the cold war since the death of Stalin in 1953, leaving Churchill the last survivor of the great alliance. So there it was again, the same theme at the end as it had been throughout his career. England and Churchill. Churchill and England. Interchangeable. One. But "sure and lasting peace" needed a time and a philosophy that have so far proved beyond the capacity of any one man or country to accomplish. Churchill could not face that far into the future. In the spring of 1955 Winston Churchill retired at last.

Graham Sutherland's Sir Winston Churchill.

Herblock in The Washington Post and Times-Herald

Burck in The Chicago Sun-

"Last act of all——."

Low, world copyright by arrangement with The Manchester Guardian

"Shh!"

Behrendt in Vrij Nederland, Amste-

"Old soldiers never die..." .

Little in The Nashville Tennessean

the British Empire . . . last for a thousand years."

Hesse in The St. Louis Globe-Democrat

"Ah-h-h-h!"

B. Z. am Mittag, Berlin

"Dropping the pilot."

Collins in The Montreal Gazette

"But what a roar!"

Culver Service.

Now he went back to his paintings and his books, his summers at Chartwell and his winters in the South of France. At long last the killing pace had eased. He moved rarely in society now, happiest in the company of either his family or of old cronies with whom he could recall more colorful days, and all the fascinating figures they had known, talk not unspiced with far-off gossip ("How much did she get out of Lord X in the end?"). On social occasions Sir Winston and Lady Churchill were given tremendous cheers by Londoners watching them step from their car to keep dinner and theater appointments. Sometimes they would visit the Old Vic to see Laurence Olivier or Richard Burton. This was not altogether an unqualified honor for the actors. Churchill knew most of Shakespeare's best speeches by heart, and he would mutter the words to himself so that the actors found themselves declaiming to the accompaniment of an audible Churchillian echo from one of the front rows center.

He showed no more disposition in his old age to grow up than he had ever done, and his love for dumb animals and living things grew even greater. Telephoning home Churchill would never fail to inquire after his dogs or his other "dear little animals." He had a due appreciation for an animal's self-respect and was not at all amused when a friend suggested an insignificant name for a new dog he had been given. "This is an important dog," he said severely.

Such operations as feeding his tropical fish became an adventure fraught with significance and emotion, a gastronomic discourse, a philosophical estimate on marine mentality. The fish were not simply fed. They were wooed with endearments. If they ate without gusto they must be ailing. Or perhaps the fish food lacked vitamins. A servant would be dispatched at full speed to telephone the servant of one of Churchill's friends who also possessed tropical fish and notes would be carefully compared as to diet, feeding times, water temperature, etc.

Philippe Halsman.

Winston at Chartwell with Rufus.

Sir Winston and Lady Churchill.

Winston Churchill was a happy man, as happy as a man could be who had so richly fulfilled his own destiny and so enjoyed the esteem of his countrymen and of humanity. There were no sorrows to take to the grave as Baldwin had done, abashed by the hatred of the nation he loved so passionately; as Lloyd George had done, obsessed with his own frustrations, hatreds and Petainist thoughts; as Neville Chamberlain had done, witnessing the destruction of every policy he had ever advocated; as Roosevelt had done, realizing too late the monstrous evil of the Russian dictator he had tried at such sacrifice to befriend. And Winston, happy in his life's record, was happy also in his home. He would play six-pack Bezique for hours with Lady Churchill, happy as a child every time he won. In his garden he would tend special flowers until he considered them beautiful enough to present to his wife.

The Churchill children were fiercely proud of and devoted to their parents. Their own lives had not been unmixed with tragedy. Sarah's first marriage ended in divorce, and her second husband, the Court photographer, Anthony Beauchamp, committed suicide. Randolph was also divorced from his first wife, though the marriage produced a son, Winston. Diana Churchill married Duncan Sandys, Minister of Defense in Harold MacMillan's Cabinet, and Mary Churchill, Christopher Soames, Secretary of State for War in the same Government. These two marriages have produced seven grandchildren for Sir Winston and Lady Churchill. Randolph, a successful journalist, has made several unsuccessful stabs at politics. A big, prematurely grey man, he guards his family like a watchdog. When a London Sunday paper announced it planned to run a series called "The Churchill Girls," Randolph announced amiably that he planned himself to write a series on the ladies in the press lord's family. The idea was hastily dropped. When another paper called him a "paid hack," Randolph sued and took the case to court. He called in support several editors who testified that Randolph, far from being a hack was independent, obstinate, pig-headed and quite impossible. In the witness box he completely crushed the cross-examining lawyer with his brilliance, won his case and collected £5,000. John Wingate, interviewer on the TV show "Nightbeat," asked Randolph a personal question about a member of his family, and was withered by a blast of abuse that blew tubes on sets across the United States. Wingate has not been quite the same since.

"Jack" Churchill, Winston's younger brother, had died in February, 1947, aged 67. Shy and retiring he had devoted his life to his stockbroking business and had shunned politics. Jack and Winston had always been on excellent terms. When Jack was bombed out in the Blitz he moved into 10 Downing Street. His wife, Lady Gwendeline Churchill, had died in 1941 and he left two sons and a daughter, Clarissa, who married Anthony Eden in 1952.

Winston still attended the House occasionally, listening carefully and politely, his hand cupped over his ear, especially when one of the younger members was talking, and although he never attempted to take part in the debate, his presence gave it a new urgency and tension. The party he had remolded went into the elections under Anthony Eden in 1955 and won by a majority of more than sixty. Winston took up again his work on *The History of the English-Speaking Peoples,* which he had set aside twenty years earlier under the pressure of politics. It did not perhaps match up to the literary Churchill at his finest. Lord Attlee, in a review, noted Winston's preoccupation with historic battles and his affection for the Cavaliers. He noted also that the space devoted to the Renaissance, Reformation, Counter-Reformation and the discovery of the New World combined was the same as that given to Henry VIII's matrimonial experiments. Attlee suggested amiably that the book might better have been called, "Things in history which have interested me." But this and similar criticism did not dim its great success.

In February, 1958, Churchill fell ill again in the south of France with pneumonia complicated by pleurisy. He was staying at the Villa la Pausa at Rocquebrune-cap-St. Martin in the mountains above Monte Carlo. His personal physician was called. Lady Churchill and his daughter Sarah were at his side. Randolph, in the United States, where he was on a lecture tour and tangling with television interviewers, was informed by telephone. So were Diana and Mary in London. From all over Europe the correspondents gathered telegraphing the grim news daily to their newspapers. They prepared solemn phrases to do justice to this era-ending occasian. The London *Mail* warned, "Pneumonia and pleurisy are bad enough in the young, but in a patient of his years they must be regarded very seriously . . . He is 83 and . . . the forces he can bring to bear are not as strong as they once were." No man could beat this score and survive, not again. And yet . . . and yet . . .

Some were reminded that Churchill had spent a lifetime brushing with illness and fighting off death. They recalled from the books—for none was so old as to remember it—that as a boy swinging in the trees in Lady Wimborne's garden at Bournemouth, he had missed his grasp and fallen thirty feet. He was unconscious then for three days and in bed for three months. His defeat at the hands of Mr. Scrymgeour (who had died in 1947) happened just after he had emerged from hospital from appendicitis and he had fought his campaign in great pain. Knocked down by a taxi on Fifth Avenue in 1932 he had stated "there was a moment . . . of a world aglare, of a man aghast . . . I do not know why I was not broken like an eggshell or crushed like a gooseberry . . ."

Death almost got him in the second World War when he went down with pneumonia twice in 1953. Then came his attack of thrombosis in 1953 which paralyzed an arm, a leg, and all one side of his body. He recovered.

Day followed day of anxiety as the book seemed at last to be closing. Then the physicians began to grow more cheerful, their

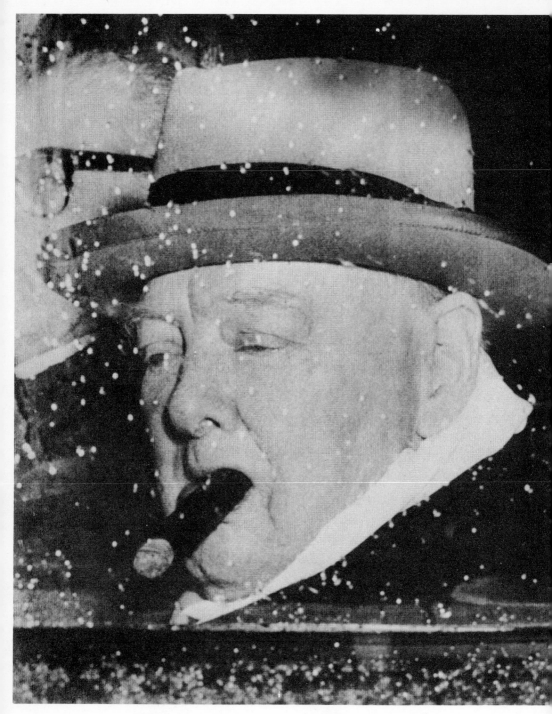

Sir Winston **Churchill** on his way home from the Riviera.

daily bulletins more optimistic. After a week his doctor announced triumphantly that Sir Winston was sitting up and attending to his correspondence. Next he stated that no further bulletins would be issued. Sir Winston had done it again.

Never was such a jig cut. It was all wrong. It did not make sense. The weather was bad and the wind howled round the *corniches*. Doom was more appropriate. The correspondents expecting to be at the death had to report recovery. It was as though mourners with white faces and dark eyes danced round the maypole, their black ribbons fluttering in the breeze. One by one the reporters departed to their bureaus in Paris to write again about the Algerian War, to London to estimate the chances of Harold MacMillan remaining Prime Minister of a fading Britain, to Bonn to discuss the problems of a divided Germany, half Communist, half free, to Washington to study the latest exchanges between Eisenhower and Khrushchev. These were the facts of a world which the old man in the mountains above Monte Carlo had survived to witness, the man who had charged with the cavalry at Omdurman and fought the Pathans in the Khyber Pass.

For a while the Riviera was left to its wintry peace. A little snow fell in Monaco. Some weeks later Sir Winston Churchill went home too. He was bundled up in a thick overcoat with a fur collar. His cigar was in his mouth. His cane was in his right hand, his left on the arm of Lady Churchill. Round, hunched, and unconquerable, he was on his way back to England. Once more he had survived to live—and perhaps to fight even—another day. "Live dangerously," he had said once. "Take things as they come. Dread naught. All will be well."

Winston Churchill

A Chronology of His Life

1874: Born on November 30.

1895: Joins the Fourth Hussars.
Serves in Cuba.

1896: Transferred to India.

1897: Attached to the 31st Punjab Infantry, Malakand Field Force.

1898: Attached to the 21st Lancers, Nile Expeditionary Force.
Takes part in the Battle of Omdurman.
The Story of the Malakand Field Force published.

1899: *The River War* published.
Defeated in June election in Oldham as Conservative.
War correspondent in Africa covering the Boer War.
Taken prisoner by Boers.
Escapes from Pretoria.

1899-
1900: } Lieutenant and war correspondent, South African Light Horse.

1900: Wins Oldham election.
Savrola published.
London to Ladysmith via Pretoria published.
Ian Hamilton's March published.

1901: Makes maiden speech in House of Commons.

1904: Breaks with Conservatives and joins Liberals.
Lord Randolph Churchill published.

1906-
1908: } Under-Secretary of State for the Colonies.

1907: Privy Councillor.

1908: Marries Clementine Hozier.

1908-
1910: } President of the Board of Trade.

1910-
1911: } Home Secretary.

1911-
1915: } First Lord of the Admiralty.

1915: Leaves Admiralty.
Resigns as Chancellor of the Duchy of Lancaster.
Leaves for France.

247

A Chronology of His Life

1916: Lieutenant Colonel commanding the Sixth Royal Scots Fusiliers.

1917-
1919: } Minister of Munitions.

1919-
1921: } Secretary of State for War and Air.

1921: Secretary of State for Air and Colonies.

1922: Companion of Honor.
Defeated in November general election at Dundee.

1923: Defeated in December general election at West Leicester.

1923-
1929: } *The World Crisis* (four volumes) published.

1924: Defeated as Independent in March election at Abbey Division of Westminster.
Returns to Conservative Party.
Wins at Epping in November general election.

1924-
1929: } Chancellor of the Exchequer.

1926: Editor of the *British Gazette* during the General Strike.

1930: *My Early Life* published.

1931: *The Eastern Front* published.

1932: *Thoughts and Adventures* published.

1933-
1938: } *Marlborough* (four volumes) published.

1936: Backs Edward VIII in abdication crisis.

1937: *Great Contemporaries* published.

1939-
1940: } Again First Lord of the Admiralty.

1940-
1945: } Prime Minister.

1945-
1951: } Leader of the Opposition.

1946: Order of Merit.

1948-
1954: } *The Second World War* (six volumes) published.

1951-
1955: } Again Prime Minister.

1953: Knight of the Garter.

Nobel Prize for Literature.

1956-
1957: } *A History of the English-Speaking Peoples* (four volumes) published.

Index

Index

Index

given command of battalion, 96; returns to political scene, 99; his inclusion in Government opposed, 99-100; is appointed Minister of Munitions, 100; becomes informed on scientific affairs, 102; is almost killed, 102; is only Englishman to receive American D.S.C., 103; heads War Office, 106; is transferred to Colonial Office, 109; his mother dies, 109; undergoes appendicitis operation, 112; loses Dundee election, 112; his political life in eclipse, 115-17; *The World Crisis* becomes best-seller, 117; loses two more elections, 119, 121; welcomed back by Conservatives, 122; is appointed Chancellor of the Exchequer, 122; puts England on gold standard, 123; workers blame General Strike on him, 126-27; becomes newspaper editor, 128-31; slams trade unions, 130; is considered England's second most powerful man, 133; resigns from Cabinet, 134; continues with his writing, 136-37; on lecture tour in United States, 137; is hit by taxi, 139; writes definitive biography of Duke of Marlborough, 139-40; warns about Hitler, 140-42; backs Edward VIII in his abdication, 146; speaks against Chamberlain's appeasement, 156; people clamor for his return, 159; joins war Cabinet, 165; is again appointed First Lord of the Admiralty, 166; warns all parties to work together, 168; becomes Prime Minister, 171; forms cabinet, 171-72; tries to bolster French, 176; inspires Munichists to work with him, 178; appeals to United States, 178; meets Roosevelt to draw up Atlantic Charter, 189-90; his friendship with Roosevelt, 190-91; falls ill with pneumonia, 192; has trouble with DeGaulle, 193-94; acts as liaison between Roosevelt and Stalin, 194; leaves for Teheran Conference, 196; collapses, 198; discord between him and United States, 202-03; at Yalta, 203-05; at Potsdam, 210; loses election, 210; resigns, 213; warns United States about Russians, 214; is given cool reception by Americans, 214-15; still heads Tory Party, 215; writes six-volume *The Second World War*, 219;

receives Nobel Prize for Literature, 219; takes serious interest in farming, 220; develops racing stable, 220; concentrates on painting, 220-223; speaks against Socialist Government, 224-25; is called warmonger, 226; declares himself for rearmament, 226-28; is Prime Minister once again, 228; accepts Order of the Garter, 230; has paralytic stroke, 232, 243; is last survivor of Big Three, 234; retires in 1955, 234; his children, 241-42; has seven grandchildren, 241; writes *The History of the English-Speaking Peoples*, 242; becomes ill with pneumonia and pleurisy, 243; survives once more, 244

Churchill, Winston (grandson), 241
Ciano, Count, 159
Clark, General Mark, 196
Clemenceau, Prime Minister of France, 64, 106-08
Cliveden Set, 142, 153, 156, 159, 178
Closing the Ring, 219
Clydesiders, "Red," 119
Colonial Office, 109-111
Colonist II, 220
Communists, 119, 140, 194, 202, 213-15, 216, 226, 244
Connaught Place, 21
Conservative Central Office, 38, 121, 142
Conservative Party, 38, 54, 56-57, 59, 62, 90, 96, 99, 111-12, 116, 121-22, 133, 142, 170, 215, 228, 234. *See also* Tory Party
Constantinople, 87
"Constitutionalist," 121
Cooper, Diana Manners, 121, 128
Cooper, Duff, 121, 128, 136, 150, 154, 156, 167-68, 171-72, 193-94
Coronation of 1953, 230-33
Crimean War, 170
Cripps, Sir Stafford, 215, 225, 226
Cromwell, Oliver, 168
Cuba, 31
Czechoslovakia, 154, 159, 160

D-Day, 198, 209
Daily Mail, 93, 126-28, 243
Daily Mirror, 172-73, 177, 226-28
Daily Telegraph, 31, 32
Daladier, Prime Minister of France, 150, 154-56
Daly's Theatre, 121

Index

Index

Index

Index

255

Index